T0095430

Journaling through

BIPOLAR
DISORDER

Journaling through

BIPOLAR
DISORDER

MAX JOSEPHS

ARCHWAY
PUBLISHING

Archway Publishing books may be ordered through booksellers or by contacting:

Archway Publishing
1663 Liberty Drive
Bloomington, IN 47403
www.archwaypublishing.com
1 (888) 242-5904

ISBN: 978-1-4808-7591-3 (sc)
ISBN: 978-1-4808-7590-6 (e)

Library of Congress Control Number: 2018912258

Print information available on the last page.

Archway Publishing rev. date: 03/18/2019

CONTENTS

PROLOGUE

I've finally decided to break off relationships with toxic people in my life: my father, my former boss who claimed to be my "friend," and another so-called "friend," Doris.

My stomach is acting up again; it must be the I.B.S. once again, and this time it really hurts--the pain, I mean. I'm not making this stuff up; it's real. Just last week I had chest pains, and we decided to go to the hospital because I thought I was having a heart attack. I was in the hospital for about 36 hours, which was just a precaution to be checked out. All was fine after all. The cardio doctor said three things to me: 1) you need to lose the weight by next year or else you could have a stroke or worse; 2) you need to join a gym; and 3) you need to get the lap band.

I have been struggling with my weight for the past seven years. I'm like a roller coaster—up and down with my weight. I'd lose a little and think I was heading in the right direction, and then bam! I'd gain it all back. What I learned is that these diets don't work; they all give you some sort of hope, but then there's little hope once you start them. For the past year, I've been on the Autoimmune Paleo Protocol Diet, and I still weigh over 300 pounds. I know a lot of the medications I take to control bipolar disorder cause weight gain, so I guess I'm screwed.

I'm a chef by trade, studied in Europe at the finest schools available. Graduated in 1983, even though my dad was sure I was going to fail and didn't hesitate to tell me so. But why would he send me to school only to fail? Doesn't really make any sense. But I did not fail; I made it through three difficult years of school. People who are toxic people suck you dry; they're rude, insensitive, and have only one agenda--theirs. They don't care about your feelings. You are, however, allowed to terminate toxic relationships, even with people to whom you are related or claim to love you. You are allowed to walk away from people who hurt you over and over. I'm finally realizing this, but it still hurts And lots of times, I still forget because I still have hope ...

CHAPTER **ONE**

My story actually begins in Germany, when in 1964, I came to the United States, along with my parents, and nine-year-old brother, Peter. I was born, in the city of Essen, which is known for being very industrial. We came to the States on the USS Berlin from Germany. My father has told me that it was a six-week journey to get to Ellis Island. My aunt, and dad's sister, sponsored our family to come to the USA. We arrived in April of 1964.

As far as can I recall, I was your average kid, just like every other kid in the United States. We lived in Chicago on the northwest side, close to a huge baseball field.

What I do remember is a great snow storm, in the winter of 1967, the snow being higher than me at the age of three. When the snow storm was over, cars were parked everywhere in the streets, like they just stopped in their tracks.

My father was a painter, and my mother was a house-wife, taking care of my brother and me.

We moved a lot, when I was younger. I remember the places, but not the streets. I do remember that once we lived in a three-floor apartment building and the neighbor next door had a black poodle name Googy, that came to our apartment every day. He was soft and furry and gave me a lot of attention when we played together. I remember being so happy to see and play with Googy, as nobody else gave me the love and attention like he did.

School was difficult for me, and what I remember about school is quite fuzzy, but I do remember that I didn't get the best grades. We spoke only German at home and in our social community, yet lessons in school were in English. My parents didn't speak English, so I didn't have anyone to help me do my homework, which made school very difficult.

I remember one specific incident about homework while attending public school. I took my homework home one day and hid it downstairs near the garbage, by the back porch. I didn't understand the work, and didn't want my father to call me stupid, or punch me in the head, like he usually did when I didn't understand something.

When I got home, my father asked me where my school books were. I simply said, there was no homework that day. I got away with that for that night; however, the next morning, when I went back downstairs to get my books, they had disappeared! The garbage men took my books and threw them away! I went to school and when my teacher asked where my books were and I replied that

I lost them, my teacher called my father and told him what had happened. I remember getting beaten by my father that night for losing the books and for lying about my homework. Yes, just another beating from my father with his belt. My mother did nothing to protect me, or maybe she didn't have a say in the matter.

My fear of my father grew each and every day. He beat me for everything, and sometimes for nothing. If I ran, he would chase me, and when he caught me he would beat me even harder. I learned to block out the pain, but the fear never left me. My father was a huge man; strong and muscular, with hands like baseball mitts. That didn't stop him from beating anyone and everyone who crossed him, including my mother.

My mother was all of five feet tall and 110 pounds, with pitch black hair and big blue eyes; she was a beauty. My father said he married her because she was the most beautiful woman he'd ever seen. Mama was a tiny woman who wanted to be perfect and have a perfect life, whatever that meant to her. She did not want to leave Germany, so she became pregnant with me so my father wouldn't force her to go to America. She didn't know my father very well, because he always got what he wanted, and when I was just 8 months old, we came to America.

My mother always loved fashion and dressing herself and her family in the very best, whether we could afford it or not. My father said she had a shopping sickness. We didn't realize until nearly 30 years later that she suffered from bipolar disorder. The illness, which was left untreated, destroyed my family.

I'm sure she was bipolar since she was quite young. Mama was born in a small town in Germany. Her mother died when she was only six years old; her father was in the military. World War II was raging all around them, with bombs dropping constantly. Mama told the story of seeing her best friend killed when a bomb dropped on her home right across the street from where my mama lived. Such devastation for a child! She told stories about taking care of her younger siblings, having no food, going door to door begging for food, and stealing potatoes from the fields to feed herself and her younger sister and brothers. I know how that influenced the rest of her life. She would never beg anyone for anything, and she would never be ashamed of not having enough of anything, including food, clothes, shoes, and jewelry.

My mother was married to my father for a total of 17 years, but not many happy years that I remember. When I was just seven years old, I vaguely remember my father beating up my mother. He had punched her in the face, full force with his fist. It all happened so fast. I remember I was sitting in a squad car, after the police of of our town tried to stop domestic violence between my dad and mom. I remember the policeman asking me if I wanted something, and I managed to ask if I could have my rabbit, which was my pet at the time. Only later, I discovered after the rabbit had been missing, that my father had taken him to the butcher shop and we ended up eating him one day for dinner. I don't remember much after that, except my mother was gone and my father started bringing home a string of women. Then one day when I was seven my parents got a divorce.

Peter married his high school sweetheart, Dianne. Peter and I tolerated each other, at that time. He was not home most of the time because he was with Dianne; I had no idea where they lived then, as I didn't visit him. I didn't know if Peter finished high school or not, but there was no graduation ceremony. I seem to remember Peter working for a security company at the time.

When I was about ten years old, Peter abused me, not sexually, but he tormented me. He would inflict pain instead. He would often be left in charge of me when my father was gone. When he tortured me as a young boy, he would make me stand for hours and not let me sit down to rest. I cried and pleaded with him to let me sit down, but he didn't care how I felt. On another occasion, I remember that he put a rope around my neck and tried to hang me from the second floor of a two-story house. Well, I'm still here, so Peter obviously failed.

One day in the middle of winter, toward evening, we were going for dinner at a burger joint. Peter was driving; he gave me money to buy food for both of us. I went inside and bought the food, as they didn't have a drive-thru, and then went outside to get back in the car. Peter was nowhere to be found. It was very cold; must have been below zero degrees. I started to cry, because he just left me there, when about ten minutes later, I saw his car in the distance driving slowly through the snow toward me. I became so angry with Peter that I threw the burgers and fries against the building. He asked me where the food was. I don't remember what I had said, but I was angry that he left me for so long. I asked him where he had gone, and he stated that he went to look for a parking spot. Three or four blocks away? I'm sure he could have parked his car by the restaurant. He had done other similar things to me, but my brain has blocked some of them. It's probably best I don't remember everything.

Around this time I was attending grade school. When I was in third grade, I had a crush on my teacher. I got lucky because I got the same teacher for the fifth grade. The only thing that I didn't like about her was that she was a smoker; maybe having so many kids in her class caused her immense pressure to smoke. This was the 70's, so it was probably the trend back then. I learned recently that she had passed away from cancer in 2009. Damn cigarettes!

I never found a reason to smoke. I remember when I was 16, while in Michigan, one of my dad's girlfriends, Darlene, had parents who lived on a farm in a small rural town in Michigan. I stayed with them in the summers when I was in my teens. I remember I had a girlfriend from the reservation there. We had many friends; and through them had my first encounter with marijuana; we smoked and it was great. I couldn't get enough of the stuff. One night when we were all high on marijuana on the reservation, we went to the farm, and being so messed up on smoking the stuff, that I stumbled through the house, looking for my boom box, and a cassette tape. I grabbed the items, and while Darlene's parents were shocked at my behavior, but they let me be and wished me a great time.

This was typical of the summers I had spent on the farm. Darlene's parents were from Germany and were hard working farmers in upper Michigan. Darlene's father had taught me how to drive the John Deere tractor around the farm. There was a river that passed through the farm. I used to walk through it with my shoes on, as I didn't want to step on the crayfish, in the river, where I built a dam near the bridge there many times by placing the large rocks at the sides of the river, making it flow faster in the middle. I remember the river passed through the farm, and the cows would drink from it. Those were such wonderful summers!

I also remember George and Elsa belonged to the Seventh Day Adventist Church, so we attended church on Saturdays instead of Sundays, when much of the town would come together for the service. I eagerly attended, because many of my friends would be there.

When I'd spend my summers on the farm, I would take the bus back to where I lived in Illinois. It was a seven to nine hour trip, but I didn't mind.

A flashback! I'm now in seventh or eighth grade, liking school, but still having a difficult time with the English language. I had special teachers, or tutors, to guide me through the writing and speech. I don't remember their names, but they were good to me. There were three schools, all on one property. One housed first to third graders, one third to fifth grades, and the other fifth through eighth graders. I was in seventh grade when I met Jack, who was my dad's girlfriend Patricia's, son. He was the same age as me, but a bit stronger. He went to a school in Chicago somewhere; I'm not sure where. We got along fine; he and his mother had a German Shepard, named Rex; a beautiful dog.

Patricia, or Pat as my dad called her, had a daughter too, but I don't remember her name. She was into a lot of creepy stuff. Jack liked hanging around me as he didn't get along very well with his sister, and didn't have a brother. As this time, I was just an ordinary kid, just like any other American kid on the block. Pat would clean for my dad at our house and he'd pay her . She had another job as a waitress at some restaurant in the city somewhere. But going back in time, Patricia was not dad's only girlfriend. At the time he also had Darlene, whom he had met after he divorced my other. Darlene was really young, in her twenties, while my dad was about twice her age. At this point in life, I know that my dad worked hard for his family, which consisted of him, Peter, and me, but Peter was married and living on his own with his wife, Diane. Peter and Dianne soon had their first child, Daniella. I remember that Peter and Dianne seemed too young to have a child so soon after their marriage, and that Peter was the only source of income for their family. Dianne didn't work, and stayed at home taking care of baby Daniella. She was a beautiful baby, as she resembled my mother, and looked like pictures I had seen of my mother when she was growing up in Germany during the post war times.

Okay, back to Jack. I don't know when this happened, but I got beat up a lot toward the end of eighth grade. Kids from all over school got involved with Jack and me; I don't even know why we were fighting. But since I was the German kid, everyone thought he should beat up the German kid, and somehow Jack got involved. He was a German kid too, which only made matters worse. We got into fights, during and after school. Back then they didn't call it bullying; I don't know what they called it. But I got clobbered every day at school. The punches hurt too. We had a lot of Jewish kids in our school. I'd go to the principal for help, but they could only do so much. I should have gotten my father involved; he would have probably beaten the crap out of all of them because that's how he solved problems. But I was very ashamed of what I was going through. At some point, I didn't want to go to school anymore. The fights got so bad at one point that they practically were in my backyard (it was only a five-minute walk to school). Jack was definitely the aggressor here; he would make them angry at me and I'd have problems at school. As a result, I did poorly in school; my grades suffered a lot, and when report card pick-up time came, I was afraid to show my grades to my father, because he would just yell and kick the shit out of me because I had poor grades. I had a terrible time with math; I couldn't understand it, and even to this day, I still don't. I got so frustrated with all the crap going on, I started to get depressed, pre high school in 1979.

My dad was not with Darlene anymore; and was now with Patricia. They were together about four or five years and so was my relationship with Jack. So when my dad's relationship broke off, so did mine with Jack. Dad had met a string of other women, and I lost count of them. I still had my mother who wanted to spend more time with me, but I only got to see her every two weeks. My father gave my mother nothing from the divorce. Bastard! She had suffered from depression when she was married to my father, during their 17 years together. He thought it was the shopping sickness. I have to admit that I had never heard of that one before, but she always had a job no matter what; she was always working very hard, no matter what job she was at. I think after my father divorced her, my mother hooked up with a guy who was on the radio; Charles, who had studied in Germany for his degree in broadcasting or journalism.

Charles was very smart and witty. My mother was very attracted to him because he had a great voice, they soon became a couple, and from him she got first-hand knowledge of a radio station. They had a radio show. Charles was also an editor for a German newspaper and was on the radio as well. I liked him a lot; he was very nice to me, and soon after, my mother moved in with Charles and they married. During this time, my father was with other women, whom I don't remember. I remember when he gave me a twenty dollar bill when I still lived at home, and told me to scram for a few hours and not to come back until dinner time. This was still in the late seventies and $20 was a lot of money for a kid.

I had met Misty, in 1981, who was my official first girlfriend in high school. I actually met her at theme park, when I dared her to go on a roller coaster ride with me. She was Italian- American, and she went to an all-girls school. I got a job in at a local gas station, across the street from her school. It was a job program with the high school that

I attended. My teacher would visit the job site and rate my job performance; the work replaced class time. I worked there for about three years, for a great boss. I had my first car, a green Plymouth, while working there. It was a plain car, and I did have to pay for the upkeep, and the gas. I don't remember having depression or any other symptoms at that time. Life was good?

Alter was my best friend in high school; we had met in gym class in my sophomore year, in the 80's. He lived in the same town with his sister and parents, about a 20-minute walk from my house. His father, Bill, was a maintenance man for buildings in the city; he was a hard worker. Alter's mother, Martha, was a homemaker. Both Bill and Martha were very kind to me. I'd often go there with Alter after school and stay for dinner. Sometimes Alter and I would go to the a local restaurant, where we would hang out with friends. They served burgers and fries and there was a game room and batting cage. Alter had an older sister, Suzanne, who went to an all-girls school too. I liked her, but it was obvious she was interested in guys other than me. But hey, I was still with my girlfriend Misty, and we were in love. What a great feeling, to know someone whom you can trust, and whose parents were nice to me. Maybe it was because I was German, who knows. Will and Phyllis, liked me a lot, so I was there often for great Italian dinners, and to see their daughter.

Then there was Bart who was a good friend of Alter, and was also German. I don't know where they met, but Bart's mom was good friends with Alter's mom, Martha, and also lived in Chicago, in a giant white house, with so many rooms you could get lost walking through the house looking for someone or something. At this point, I was still friends with Jack, so introduced him to Alter. Jack was going to a high school where you need at least a 3.5 grade point average to be admitted; definitely a school for smart guys only. Alter was going to an all-male high school in the city, but then transferred to a local school when his parents moved. So that was pretty much most of my friends.

When I was in my junior year in high school, my father had asked me what I'd wanted to do for a living or a career. I needed to think a little, and then I came up with that I wanted to be a chef. Dad thought about it, knowing very well that I wasn't good at math and being a chef was more about recipes, memory of ingredients, and hard work. He agreed to the idea and got in touch with Charles, my mother's husband, who knew people in the German hotel industry, including a hotel manager. This hotel was one of the leading hotels in the world, and was rated tenth best in 1983. I was still a German citizen, and getting a job with the hotel as a German was not going to be a problem. So after high school, I was to go directly to Germany, to start my apprenticeship as a cook there. I was to start school in Munich in September of 1983.

So where was I going to live, while at the German hotel? My father called up my aunt Christine who lived in a small city, about 40 miles away from where I would be studying. He told her what he was planning where I was concerned, and that he needed her help. She agreed to help me with school and my living arrangements. My first residency would be in a town close to Aunt Christine and my second would be in Munich. At the time, however, I didn't know my dad was paying for me to live there with my aunt.

Many years before this, I would get a small package every year from Aunt Christine (my mother's sister), and my mom told me it was a special present from Aunt Christine. Many years went by without me ever knowing who she really was, and her connection to all this. I do know that Aunt Christine always thought of me as a family member, even though she had three children of her own--Benny, Stefanie, and Anna. Benny was close to my age, and we got along quite well. Anna was sweet and we got along well, too. I never had a sister, and she was sharp as a whistle . Every time I did something wrong, she called her mama (Aunt Christine). I believe that with a family--a real family--and I had a lot of catching up to do. I was twenty years old, yet I never really what it meant to be part of a real family! But Anna kept me in shape, since I was the new family member.

Aunt Christine accepted me right away into their family; Uncle Ray was the head of the household, and worked as a principal at one of the schools in town. He and I got along quite well, better than I had thought we would; he was very quiet and stern but gentle, not like my father at all. He would retreat into the cellar of the house, where he had a room filled with his vision, his stuff, and where he could escape the daily grind of family living and a rigorous job. I remember he loved the national soccer team and they were in the spotlight of the soccer world at that time.

Even though Benny and I got along well, we had a weird sort of language barrier, because he spoke with a Bavarian dialect which I didn't understand.

Just before going to Germany, I had gone to a special school to sharpen my German language skills. So before I would go to Germany, I would have a little more knowledge about the language and its people.

So in September of 1983, I was moving back to Germany, at age 20, so I could go to school and become a chef. The program would take about three years total. At that time I couldn't be out of the country for more than a year, because I was a German citizen living in the USA. So when I had summer vacation in Germany, I would go back home for six weeks, and then go back to Germany and start the second season of my apprenticeship. Aunt Christine would type up weekly notes on what I had accomplished in a week at school. I also had to write down what I learned at school in a week. I took French, German, English, Religion, and Practical Skills in the Kitchen, and then I had to write what I did at the hotel, like make Eggs Benedict or scrambled eggs, and explain the process of how I did that. The writing had to be typed in perfect German, and the Executive Chef and the School Master had to write his name on the weekly notes to confirm he read the notes..

On my first day of orientation, I met a guy from Chicago, whose father owned a German restaurant. Matt was his name, and he had gone to school not far from where I grew up.

I also met a guy named Martin, who was from a

university town. I got along so well with him that he ended up going with me to Chicago on our first-year vacation from the hotel and school, and for each vacation for the entire three years. He didn't speak with an accent; he had lived in Finland for a while and spoke their language quite well. When he'd visit with me at home, he spoke like a regular American. He loved Chicago, especially the downtown area, where all the shopping was, and he especially liked the sport teams. We had a great friendship developing. I was very happy too, to have a friend who really understood me so well. It was like we grew up together, and knew everything about the other person, both likes and dislikes.

Matt was working at the Hotel as a Commis de rang, in a different part of the hotel than I was. He was already an accomplished chef and we had a lot in common.

Then there was Doris, who was one of the most toxic persons I'd ever met. We met at a group that I was hosting in 2012-2013. The meeting was at a restaurant. She was 20 years older than I and from Germany, also. We would get together at nearby coffee shops with, John, a mutual friend. Doris was constantly talking about moving back to Germany, or anywhere except staying in the States. We would have discussions about conspiracy theories, and almost every topic one could think, but she often times would put me down as a person.

As time went on, I began to hate her for saying things to me, or that my wife was no good for me, and that I could do better. Doris didn't like the way I dressed. Even worse, when she learned how much money my wife, Alicia, made she kept holding it over my head. When I'd say I didn't have any money to go out with, Doris would get angry and say my wife made so much money as a teacher, so how could I be broke?. Doris was constantly putting me down, telling me how to dress, becoming a psychopath. I don't know how John put up with her; but he was a good friend to me, and I to him.

I later formed another social group via the internet and Doris joined it. At first we would meet at various restaurants in the area, and would either talk in German or English, and talk mostly about the food. Being the host and organizer was quite stressful, as a lot of people would RSVP and then not show up, which would frustrate many restaurant owners because they had reserved tables for us, and would end up turning others away. The group would cost about 80 dollars a month, and it was difficult to get sponsors to donate anything. I started the club because of my interest in German foods and its rich culture, and since I was a chef, I thought it would be a great idea. It really wasn't.

CHAPTER **TWO**

Okay, back to Doris. Alicia and I were married about 13 years when I met Doris. Still, Doris would always put my wife down, especially when my Alicia wasn't there to defend herself. I took it as my job to honor my wife, and not to give in to Doris. However, because of my own issues, I was very intimidated when it came to defend my wife and just nodded to Doris in agreement instead of objecting to whatever she said. I knew though, that Alicia was better than that. She was definitely a better person than Doris. Perhaps Doris just hated other women, because she said to my wife one day that, " all women are bitches". I guess she didn't want any woman to be her friend, and especially Alicia. The two of them would get along from time to time, at my urging, only to have Doris say something cruel about Alicia once again. Alicia only tolerated Doris for me because she thought Doris was a good friend to me. I didn't tell Alicia all the nasty stuff Doris said about her or about me. Once, when Doris said something so mean to me, putting me down in the process, I told her I wished John put a muzzle on her mouth to shut her up. I kept thinking that moving away from Doris would make it easier for me to breathe normally again.

Then there was my father. I won't say his name, because that's all he is, my father, another very toxic person. It must run in the family, because his sister was so much like him. To this day, both of them would like nothing better than to see my mother suffer, who is now in memory care for Lewy Body Dementia. She is doing as well as can be expected, and will be 85 next spring. I love my mother with all my heart; she has been so kind to me over the course of my life, unlike my father. Nobody can say anything bad about her; she is an inspirational person to me and to my wife.

I think my father and his sister are one and the same—pure evil. I never had a good relationship with my aunt, as I always had to prove my self-worth to her and to her children, who are a little younger than me. Her daughter banned me from going to her wedding because I was bipolar. Like I would have been a threat? I also never had a good relationship with her other children, so this may be the extent that I will talk about them. My aunt always looks scary mean; I always had to walk on eggshells around her, and it seems that no matter what I said, it was never good enough for her because I was bipolar, so I must be crazy.

My father was someone I could never figure out. He

treats me like crap most of the time. I was never going to be good enough for him to be proud of me, no matter how hard I tried, or what I accomplished. Like when I went to culinary school in Germany, he expected me to fail. Whereas a real father would be proud of his son for even trying.

Okay, moving on, I am getting to emotional when I think of him now and how he has destroyed anything left for me.

I have—or had—an older brother, Peter. Although Peter is still alive, as far as I know, he is dead to me. I actually do have pictures of when we were younger, and were together, which would suggest that we had a good relationship at one time. But what little we had was destroyed when I said something quite cruel to him, about ten years ago. I told him that he was a horrible father, and that I could do a better job raising his daughter, Daniella than he could. I also went on to add what kind of person I thought he had become. I was off my medications and really laid into him, but what I said was the way I truly felt and thought. As a result, we don't speak to each other anymore. At the time, my mother was really helpful, and explained to me a week later that after what I said to Peter, and that he couldn't sleep all week because of it. Perhaps this was an act on his part, and using what I said for a good reason not to speak to me anymore. But what I didn't understand, is that his wife was a nurse, so she should have had knowledge of the medical field and bipolar disorders. How could she live with someone who was so mean and heartless? She did, however, seem to like my wife, and they ran into each other a few times, and were cordial to each other. From the first meeting, though, Alicia had a bad feeling about Bonnie and didn't want anything to do with her. Peter, however, has become very much like my father. I think they have the same personalities; they both were born in June, their birthdays just a few weeks apart. My father always wanted to be right about something, the other person was always dead wrong, and you didn't dare say anything to him to the contrary. I wasn't going to talk so soon again about my father, but the negativity just seems to always rear its ugly head at me.

Just earlier today, my wife and I were on our way to the fitness club, ready to do some healthy exercise, when I really felt weak about something, and my chest felt like it was being crushed, and my breathing was getting more shallow. I got so emotional, and couldn't control my feelings when thinking about certain toxic people. They just suck the breath out of you and leave nothing for you to live for sometimes. Yes, I had a fleeting thought about Doris again. Alicia and I were driving to the fitness club and she was chatting about her work, co-workers, and the name Doris came up. I thought of toxic Doris, and got so angry and felt like I was losing control. I was getting very irritable and told Alicia to stop talking. I told her she had to drive, that I couldn't handle it anymore. Later, I told Alicia I was sorry and wanted to continue driving, which I did, but I didn't want to talk about Doris anymore, as she is a selfish person, whose only goal is to make others as miserable as she was. I still did not tell Alicia all the nasty things Doris had said about her or me.

I do have one more thing to say about Peter. At one point Peter had helped me do my taxes, which year I do not remember, and at that time he must have taken my social security number and used it for his own personal gain. Peter works for a government office. I believe he used the information for himself to get a credit card, because he had to prove residency and wasn't an American citizen. By using my social security number, it would help him get a credit card, as I was out of the county. I did learn, though, from my father that Peter was using my social security number, because he said Peter was "improving my credit score". Also, Peter's ex-wife had told me later that he was planning to use my social security number.

Peter still has not come up with an acceptable reason as to why he hasn't visited my ailing mother. It makes me so angry that he hasn't had the time to visit his own mother, who raised him as a child to a full-grown man. His wife stops by on occasion, as I have seen in the log that I have to sign at the entrance of the building. I have heard that she introduces herself to people as a nurse to impress them, but they just laugh at her.

They had better all treat my mother with respect, because my mother has the memory of a child, as she forgets about every five minutes who she is. My mother was the greatest person ever to be on the radio for 31 years; she entertained, mentored, and to the last day, wowed people with her perfect style on the radio. She even had received several awards from the mayor and others. But one award she was really excited about was the medal of honor, which she still remembers well and what it stands for. I remember her telling me about it when my father divorced her. She had the heart, soul, and beauty of a wonderful person; she always treated my wife, Alicia, with respect. She loves Alicia as her own daughter.

My mother would always have a surprise for us when we would visit her at her home before she developed dementia. Her home was like a perfect model home; a museum. She would record her radio show from her room, in a special room in her house, where I lived in the garage for a while. She was married to her fifth husband for about 17 years, who was a famous soccer player for an amateur club, and would sometimes do commercials for mama on the radio. He had a deep voice, which mama liked. I had lived there with them back in 1995, when I was suffering from severe depression, after being put into a mental facility in Germany by my ex-fiancée Tanya, whom is another toxic person.

Yeah, what a time that was. I was in a mental facility, and I wanted to go back to America after spending a year in the hospital for depression. I had called my father and asked him if I could live with him, and his response was that I was too sick to stay with him. He had a huge house at the time and was living there alone. There would have been plenty of room for me to crash, until I got on my feet again.

After that, I called my brother, Peter, and asked him if I could live with him and his wife, and he told me no as well. I don't remember the reason, but that was a dead end for me too. So, finally I had called my mother, and she had said yes, but only under her rules. I'd rather take my mom with rules than have no place to stay at all.

Getting back to America was a bit of a problem as I had no money, except for a little savings account through a small bank. I requested a credit card through the bank, which took about two weeks to receive, even though I ordered it express shipping. At this point, I was still living at the hospital. My finance at the time, Tanya, had me removed from our condo, and had declared me mentally incompetent by a judge. She was angry at me that it had gone this far, and thought I was the devil in disguise, although I really did nothing to provoke her. At this time, I had still not being diagnosed with bipolar disorder and she didn't understand what was wrong with me.

Meanwhile, I was basically living out of a suitcase at the mental hospital from which I was allowed to leave in the mornings to go to the daily clinic by bus. After lunch, patients were allowed to take a nap. I took advantage of the time and snuck off to the bank where I had a savings account to see if the credit card had arrived, and discovered that it did. Everything was within walking distance, thank goodness, in this little city. The name of the town means "House of God," so I was in a good place to start.

Before I got really sick with severe depression, I had

met with a doctor who was from South America, and who told me that my illness isn't measured by days and weeks, but is measured by months and years. I began to cry, knowing that I'd never get out of there, and not being free as a bird. I believe I called the American Consulate and told them I was being held as a hostage in a hospital. They didn't believe me; so much for being an American citizen. Anyway, I was put into this special mental hospital by Tanya, who thought it was best for me.

As I write this, I can feel the stress, pain, and fatigue that happened over 20 years ago. It all seems so real, so near, instead of in the past.

The reason I made Tanya believe that she had to put me into that facility was that I had told her that I had the cure for cancer; to get a hold of seeds from an apricot and to crush them down to a powder. She really thought I was off my rocker. And what I wanted to do with this information sounded even crazier yet, as I wanted to go to Holland and tell the king and queen of my new idea to cure cancer! Of course, I never had a chance to go because I was in in a town far away, by myself, with no means of transportation. But now my luck had changed because my new credit card had arrived at the bank and it had four thousand Deutsche marks on it, which was about $3,600. This could help me get to Aunt Christine's home. I always wondered why no one had asked to talk to me for the entire year; not Christine, not my parents, or even my American friends. Tanya had told everyone I was doing fine and all was well. They had no idea of what was really going on or that I had been hospitalized for a year. .

I didn't know that my family was sending money to Tanya, because I was not working at the time. I believed that my parents sent about four hundred dollars each--which would be about eight hundred a month—to Tanya! What she did with the money, I'll never know because I never saw a penny of it. Now I had the perfect opportunity to go back to American and go back home; I had a credit card with enough funds on it to get me back.

First, I tried to call Aunt Christine, to tell her that I was coming to visit her. It was about 400 miles by car to her house. I could make it in a day. So that next day I went to a car rental place and booked a car, a one-way trip. I asked for a car big enough to fit my six-foot-plus frame comfortably during the trip. I hadn't thought about the daily clinic or the hospital at all. They would know that I was missing after a day or two. I just wanted to escape and be on my way back home. So I started driving to Aunt Christine's home, but only to discover that I was going the wrong way, after driving about 100 miles. There are few signs in Europe that tell you if you are travelling in the right direction. You just had to know, and plan ahead. I stepped on the gas, and drove about 100 miles an hour. When I got to my aunt's house, I was confused, and parked the car near a park, got out, and locked the keys in the car! I called the rental car company from a telephone booth. The person on the other end of the phone was upset and yelled at me to bring the car back to them! I just hung up and managed to get to a train station close by and checked the schedules. I got on a train to the main train station and called my aunt. Uncle Ray came to pick me up.

I thought he was one of the good guys, someone I could trust. I remember he picked me up in his older model dark green, four-door sedan. When I got to my aunt and uncle's home, for some strange reason, Peter and his wife were there too, visiting. I told Peter that I was on vacation and that I was going to the States to visit our mother. He seemed to think nothing of it, especially since he turned down my request to live with him.

Bastard, I thought. Can't help out his only brother.

I told Aunt Christine about the whole lie, that I was really leaving the hospital to go back home to live with mama. For some reason, I thought my aunt already knew everything, or that Tanya was conspiring with her the whole time. Hey, maybe they even split the money between them. I really didn't know anymore what to expect.

My wife just called me, and asked me a serious question-- if I would still be home when she got here, and I said definitely yes. I guess I have been acting strangely? Alicia has been through so much!

Aunt Christine and Tanya became friends after I introduced them, back in 1990. I'm very sure that Tanya knew I was going to Aunt Christine's. But that's all she really knew, because my trip still was about going home to the United States. I was very certain of that. So I was very careful not to mention to Aunt Christine that I was going home for good. I did tell her I was going on vacation to the United States to visit family, although I'm sure she called Tanya right away and told her what I was up to.

I bet they're still wondering where I got the money.

I stayed a few days with my aunt and made plane

reservations to go America. I learned that a round-trip ticket was cheaper than a one-way ticket. I still had the credit card with me, and all else I had with me was a suitcase full of clothes, my teddy bears from when I was a child, my passport, and my German driver's license. Tanya still had all my personal belongings, which I never saw again. To this day, I never got anything back. Even though the condo we bought and everything inside it belonged to both of us, she kept everything.

So, there I was, ready to begin a new life in America again, in the summer of 1995. I was going to live with my mother and her husband.

I still felt like I had to tell my Aunt Christine where I was going.

Peter and his wife were there on vacation as they wanted to visit tourist attractions. Peter hadn't notified me that he was coming to Germany. Oh well, another toxic person in my life who doesn't deserve my trust or anything else, even though he is my brother. I'm sure my father knew that Peter was coming to Germany and that he wasn't letting me know that he was. Sometimes, I wondered if I really was family to them.

I asked Uncle Ray to drive me to the airport a few days later. It was only about 50 miles away, and with no posted speed limit, we were there very quickly.

My mother was very excited to see me when I arrived at the gate. We had to take a cab back to her car, at the hotel, where she had parked. The parking fees at the airport were outrageous. We drove together to her home . Her beautiful home was cozy and safe. She had bought a bed for me to sleep on; it was a twin bed, which was okay by me. She had the bed placed on the second floor where the fax machine was located. Although it was afternoon, it was still quite dark, so I could take a nap. It felt so good to have a place I could call home.

My mother went over the rules that I was to adhere to while living in her house. I could not leave the house in the middle of the night; no playing loud music or making noises while she was sleeping. Mama was very sensitive to sound and could not sleep if there were noises in the house. Her house was actually a townhouse; there were three townhomes very close together, and you could hear your neighbors' TVs playing in the background. It drove me crazy to hear noise when I was trying to sleep. I guess I must be as sensitive as my mother was about sound. It made me very irritable quickly, but I never discussed it with my mother while living there. I had to stay busy so I didn't drive my mother crazy while she was working in the house on her radio show. Her husband had his own job, so he was gone from early morning to late evening.

The most difficult thing for me was being off my medications for over six to eight weeks. The last time I had any medication was in the hospital. I felt horrible. Why had I come to America?

Oh, yes, I was there to visit my mother. Being off the medication made me forget why I came there in the first place. I was on 100 mg. of a very strong medication in liquid and tablet form. I was oh, so fried in my brain; I would tell my mom why I needed the meds and if I didn't get them soon, that I would wind up harming myself. Or maybe I didn't really say it, but it is how I felt. That type of medication is very harmful to people like me, but the first thing I had to do was to find a doctor, or a psychiatrist, to prescribe the medication. We found a doctor, but also found that without insurance, the meds were quite expensive. We were able to use cash, though, and so got a 30-day supply of my medicine which cost $100 a month. Now, this doctor is only giving me what I told him I needed; there are probably other good meds as well, but I wasn't sure what.

The medication made me feel a little better, though. My mother had paid out a lot of cash for me so far, but she said she was doing it out of love.

Then I was looking for a job as a chef or sous chef, which is what I was doing in Europe before I had been hospitalized.

Somehow, Tanya knew that I had arrived back in the States. Oh great, now she knows where I am. I didn't want her to know, and I'm sure Aunt Christine told her of my plans. Tanya and I had the German version of the American Express card, on which we owed about four thousand German marks. She told the credit card company exactly where I was, and they came after me, even though some of it was her responsibility. She had German lawyers contact me and more or less said that if I didn't pay, I'd be in a whole lot of trouble. At first, I didn't want to tell my mother about this, but then when I did, she was fuming that Tanya would do that to me. I didn't have the money, so my mother paid the bill which was about $2,600, by check to the credit card company.

Tanya seemed to want to get even with me for leaving her. However, when I was in the hospital, she couldn't care less about me. Now, all of a sudden, I was important to her. I had actually talked to her on the phone for a few moments when she called, and she told me that she was angry that I left for America, like I left her there. She doesn't even like it in the States, so why would she care? Sure, Aunt Christine must have been involved.

It was a couple of weeks before I could find a job; my mom knew someone at the local drug store, and got me a job there. I had to wear a clean-collared shirt with tie, dark pants, and dark shoes. My mind couldn't even begin to start working full time, so the job only lasted two days. I couldn't concentrate, my medication wasn't right, and I was having mood swings, which made me quite irritable.

Since the job at the pharmacy wasn't really working for me, my mother contacted a friend who owned a company that made molds for aircraft parts. Her friend agreed to hire me and I got an apprenticeship there as a mold maker. I remember that year well--1996. I'd have to get up very early in the morning to begin a ten-hour day; I also worked on Saturdays at least four hours. After work, most everyone went to a health club that was primarily for employees. The fees for the club was taken out of one's paycheck. There I met a lot of employees who knew my parents and treated me as a friend, or family.

I'm not quite sure how this happened, but my mother got me an apartment at a very nice building not far from her home. It was a clean one bedroom and it was perfect for me.

Mama was paying for a the apartment and my car. When I'd get my paycheck, I'd give it to my mother and she would take care of my bills, which included the one-bedroom apartment. Mama had also bought all my furniture for the apartment. She said she just wanted me to be happy, which I was then.

My mother was still working at the radio station, which was her passion, along with her husband. I was working as an apprentice, driving the company truck to various places to get various parts for clients. I was trusted at the company, and for that I was thankful, and thankful that I had a job. I also was required to go to school and study geometry, at the local community college. Being that my math skills weren't too good, they gave me options for math classes I could take, but nothing seemed to help. They then had to let me go at work, because math was a big part of the company's success. My mind was spinning and I couldn't concentrate at school or at work. I was still on the wrong medication.

One great thing did happen to me though, while working at this company, was that a man (I do not remember his name) introduced me to these tapes for self-improvement. I have some of the tapes that I still listen to. I'm grateful to my friend for helping me find these and I think of him when I listen to them today.

I was beginning to feel that life was really grand, and that one should make the most of it, because being alive is wonderful. The Lord gave me life, and I should live it. Unfortunately, I really didn't take it like I should have when I was trying to kill myself again, with the meds that made me feel suicidal. I made two attempts, and thank God they failed, or I wouldn't be writing this book. One time, I remembered that I had slit my wrist because I wanted my mother's attention. The police were called and I went to the hospital for the wounds to my wrist, which were life-threatening. Another time, I was very depressed and tried to kill myself through affixation. Again, this was a failed attempt.

I'm still here!

I blame the drug companies for making those drugs available in the first place. It doesn't matter what drug; they all had bad side effects. After the second attempt, I was put into a mental health facility and I was awaiting transfer to another facility, which turned out to be hell. I had no rights there, whatsoever.

Interesting, but it seemed that for those who did not have insurance, they would be kept longer in a facility. I don't know why that was. Also, they rationed cigarettes to people who would then went outside and smoke. I pretended to be a smoker, just so I could go outside and feel the cool air on my face. When in actuality, I really didn't care to smoke at all.

I also remember dating someone at the time; her name was Melissa, and we met through a dating service through the newspaper. I had put in ad in that said something like "European trained chef, who speaks German." I met Melissa in 1997. She was very pretty—round face, curly light brown hair, and tall. She reminded me of Betty Boop, who was her favorite cartoon character. We hit it off right from the start. She was of German descent, and spoke some German, too. Melissa worked for a major hotel in the suburbs as a catering sales manager; she lived in the city. We were together for a little over a year. I did love her, but the problem was that we had a hard time controlling the negative things that eventually drove us apart.

Life is so simple, so why are there problems?

I guess it was my fault. I would create a problem for no reason, and then dwell on it. My memory is a bit fuzzy as to where I was living at the time. I think I was still living at my mom's place when I met Melissa, and then I was renting a room in someone's house, next to the highway. The room was $400 monthly, and was only ten minutes away from my other job. There was a guy whose room was next to mine, and he'd work nights and kept me up a lot, as he was so noisy. The owners of the house had a baby whose nursery was right above my room. I heard the baby crying all night, footsteps as the parents went to calm her. I was going crazy with all the noise and lack of sleep.

My mother once surprised me with a tiny refrigerator, which just fit into my small room to keep milk and a few other things cold. My mother was always so good to me, throughout her whole life. She may have told me that I was costing her a lot of money, but she always said that I was worth every penny. She did like Melissa at first. Then my relationship with Melissa broke down. Melissa said she had loved me, but that I destroyed it all. I remember that I told her that I wished she never would have depression in her life, and she replied that she would never have what I had. It did make me feel like crap. I didn't ask for this damn illness.

I just remembered that I did have a relationship with another girl, with the same first name. I will call her Melissa Two. I had met her through my mother's friend. My mom introduced us at her friend's party. Melissa Two was cute, short, and a little chubby, but I got along with her right away. I still had the one-bedroom apartment and I was still working as an apprentice. Melissa Two lived in a very upscale suburb. Her parents were hard workers; her father owned his own metals company. They were nice to me and I was good to their daughter. Her parents owned a summer place where we would go to relax. I loved riding the jet ski the most! We would have grilling parties, with Melissa's father being the grill chef. I think that Melissa also had an older brother. My mama wanted me to marry Melissa because her parents were well off, and she thought that maybe I could get a job working for her father at his company. But I wasn't in love with her, and that's why we broke it off. I still wished her lot of luck in finding someone.

Later, I worked for a different company as a chef. They made huge nuts and bolts for aircraft carriers. I worked there from 1997 to 1999. I think I found the job in the newspaper for a chef to help in the kitchen during breakfast and lunch. The executive chef was Brad . I'll never forget him; he made it so difficult for me to get a decent raise for working my ass off. Promises, promises. I put hard sweat into the place. I loved coming to work, and started early in the morning because the doors opened for breakfast at five-thirty. I was in the front of the line most of the time, had direct contact with the employees of the company who came for breakfast, lunch and snacks, and they all got to know me by my first name. I really worked hard at this place, and was proud that I had a great job and felt important. I made good friends with another who was a prep cook, and who also worked her butt off for Brad. He is also a toxic person. I didn't need his friendship, but I worked for the bastard for two years and he just knocked me down; he knew that I suffered from bipolar illness and he took advantage of my weakness. He promised me raises, but never delivered. When I reported it to the head of personnel, Brad said I lied and they believed him.

CHAPTER **THREE**

It's time we talked more about Tanya, and who she was in my life. I met Tanya back in Germany, and would see her during the many summers that I would go to Germany and stay with my grandparents on my father's side. She was my grandfather's neighbor, and her father worked with my grandfather. As youngsters, we'd play in the sandbox together.

We were probably about eight to ten years old at the time. My grandfather and his wife were so good to me. I recently learned that she had died in 2009 from dementia at the age of 92. I loved her dearly, and tried to call her often, but her hearing was diminishing, so we had a difficult time talking on the phone.

Every other year or so, when I traveled to Germany (1983, 1985, 1989, 1990, 1993, 1995, 2006, and 2008), I would see Tanya, as she would manage to get in touch with me. During 1989-1990 I was working for an airline as a chef in their wide-body kitchens on the airfield at the largest, busiest airport in Illinois. I received a job offer while there from a hotel in Europe when I was asked to translate for visiting chefs. They were impressed with me and asked me to return to Germany and work with them. What an honor!

My father was pushing for me to take the job in Germany but I was caught between a rock and a hard place. I wanted to stay in America because they paid me very well, and my best friend Alter was also working for the airlines as a bagger. If I stayed, I would have had a great future with them. But I listened to my father—again—and moved to Germany in September of 1989. That was the beginning of the end for me.

I was a Commis de Cuisine—just a fancy name, doesn't mean I earned much, but I was just there to get experience, and learn as much as I could. The job lasted about 11 months, as my bipolar illness got in the way of me becoming the best chef that I could be. I had a difficult time working with the other chefs there, and they, in turn, were giving me a hard time, while the executive chef was expecting more from me and I couldn't deliver. I because very depressed there. It seemed like I took a bigger leap than I could handle with this job, as I was just messing up all the time. I asked the hotel director if I could have a different job there, so I became the beginning waiter of the main restaurant. I was still having a difficult time and didn't think I could hold on to this job much longer.

The personal chef said to me one day that he would have to release me because I wasn't pulling my own weight, and other people had to step up to assist me in my duties. I managed to get a short letter of recommendation from them, however. I did get something really cool from the hotel—I got a golden coin, and a large book from the hotel about the hotel. I ended up going back to Chicago with my head down because I had failed at this job. Still, being on no medication, or the wrong medication, was destroying my life.

As expected, my father was upset with me because and he made sure that I knew that I had failed and made me feel like crap. Depression started in again, and I felt worthless and completely alone. I didn't know where to go from there; I needed to gather myself together and start completely over. I lived at my father's house for a while, so I could get back on my feet. I found a new job at a catering company. They paid me well as a kitchen cook. The owners and the executive chef liked me, but I had a fallout with the sous chef. However, within three years, I moved up quickly to catering steward. The owners trusted me; I was doing my job to the best of my ability. I also was the head party chef for catered events in the area. This is where Tanya came back into my life.

Tanya and I were calling each other every week, and were talking about her coming to visit. We were getting closer; she was sort of my childhood sweetheart from my summer visits to Germany. She had her own beauty, which I really adored. I think we were falling in love with each other, so the summer of 1993 was the first year that she came to visit me. I still had to work, but made as much time to see her as I could.

I lived close to the beaches; only a half-hour walk away to the nearest beach from my apartment.

She finally arrived. She spent her entire six-week vacation with me. When Tanya came back in the summer of 1993, we made plans for me to move back to Germany. I talked to my bosses at the catering company; they wanted me to be sure that this is what I really wanted. I was making good money, but I wanted to go. I got excellent letters of recommendation from the executive chef, president, and vice president of the catering company; yet it made me feel sad that I was leaving such a great company. I wished them all the success of the future, and left on great terms.

I talked to my parents about my decision, and they were happy for me, but my mother was at the same time quite sad because I was going back to Germany again after all the problems I had had in the past. I told my parents that I was in love with Tanya and I wanted to be with her.

━━

After I arrived in Germany, Tanya and I lived in a dorm at the school she attended. I then needed to look for a job. My first job was with a hotel, located near the main train station where the director offered me a job in sales as a food buyer for the hotel. I worked there for about nine months until once again the depression set in. It seemed that every time I landed a great job, my depression would get in the way of something great. Just bad timing?

Then in 1994, I got a great job at a French hotel chain in the center of the city. I worked there for a while as a sous chef for the main hotel, and later transferred to one of its other divisions, that catered to a pharmacy company on the outside of the city. I'd take a company bus to get there; the hours were great. Monday through Friday and some weekends with parties. The executive chef was a great chef, and liked my style of cooking as well.

One weekend, a group of us were playing soccer, and since I had bronchitis, I collapsed on the soccer field, and was taken to the local hospital. From what I had heard about my condition, I had a double lung collapse and was in a coma for about 11 days. I was really in bad shape. My mother, and Peter, came to Germany and were at the hospital; my father didn't come, said he had to work. No, I wasn't doing too good. Aunt Christine came to see me as well. I was given a 2% chance of surviving, it looked like the end was near for me.

Then poof! I suddenly woke up! With the help of the hospital personnel, I finally got on my feet again. The first person I remember seeing was Tanya. I was so happy to see her, and to be alive at the age of 29, definitely too young to die. I remember that as I awoke, my sight was kind of fuzzy, and I couldn't see clearly at first. What I saw was something red, and then I realized it was Tanya. I thought that I had died and gone to heaven. Tanya told me how happy she was that I was alive and well. She told me how difficult it was for her to see me with all the monitors and tubing attached to my body; she didn't think I was going to survive. She told me I had had a double lung collapse, and that the doctors couldn't figure out what was wrong with me, and weren't sure what to do.

I stayed in the hospital for another few weeks, so they could make sure that all my organs were functioning properly, and that I wouldn't have a relapse.

Tanya and I told the doctors at the hospital that our apartment had high humidity. It was later discovered that there was mold growing on the walls that I was inhaling and breathing in the mold spores. That had made me sick with the bronchitis and led to further complications. Then I was running in the rain while playing soccer. Now I had asthma.

I still have asthma today, and while I am writing this, it is acting up; I'm coughing and starting to feel dizzy. I understand that this cough can very well be psychological, and the more I write about my past experiences, the more ill I feel. Most doctors would give you a pill for this problem.

This writing is definitely getting to the core of my body. I feel weak sometimes as though I cannot continue, but my inner drive is pushing me forward, and a voice keeps telling me to keep writing, and not to stop. I know that there really is a reason why I had so many near-death experiences, but somehow, I just seemed to beat the odds so many times. I believe that the Lord wanted me to write this and make a statement to everyone out there. He is speaking through me, and I'm telling you that He does exist, and He loves us all—each and every one of us. You can be saved; we have the right to exist.

I'm not making this stuff up. I was baptized Mormon

in the 1990's. I remember two men from the Church of Latter Day Saints near my apartment. They approached me and started talking about God and their own beliefs, and the message He was trying to convey to me. I went to the Mormon church and I really felt special that day; I felt like I was finally going home to God's kingdom. It felt wonderful—amazing, and exhilarating.

My parents never had me baptized when I was a child, and left it up to me to choose. For some reason, though, my wife and I haven't been in church for quite some time. This could be the mark of the beast keeping us away. Soon, we'll go back to God's kingdom, and honor Him the way I did before.

———

Okay, back to earth. After I got out of the hospital, I couldn't get my job back; the position had been given to someone new. It had been a total of eight weeks that I had been in the hospital, and the company couldn't hold the position open for me. So, I decided to take some time off and rest a bit. But I didn't stay healthy for long, as in 1994, I had my first bout with manic depression. My first episode was one year to the date of my double lung collapse.

I started to arrange things differently around the house, and everything just had to be perfect. I had no idea what was happening to me, and Tanya, whom I was still living with, was asking me some weird and funny questions. She asked me if I was changing the way I felt about her, and once mentioned that was the devil's work. So, she told me she made an appointment with a well-known doctor at the hospital, but actually, she tricked me. I thought I was there for an illness and she had me already committed to the mental facility. There is nothing I hate more than being tricked. So much for the trust between two adults who supposedly loved each other. So immature; yet we were both about 30 years old at that point.

Another memory!

Back in Chicago and Father's Day was approaching, so I went to the Chicago Cubs ticket office early one day to buy two tickets to the Cubs game for Father's Day. When I asked my father to come with me, he refused, and said he wasn't going to waste his time at a stupid ballgame with me. I just wanted some father-son time together. It didn't matter to him, though. I went alone to the game.

CHAPTER **FOUR**

Okay, back to Executive Chef, Brad. I had worked with him for about three years now. I had broken the relationship off with Melissa One. It was a bad break-up. I can't remember what she had told me toward the end—something like I destroyed the relationship all on my own. I was really sad because I had really loved her. But it doesn't matter what I think now. It's over and that is that. I believe it was 1997; work was getting more difficult for me. I was getting more responsibility, and the chef kept promising me a raise. This was going on for about three months.

Meanwhile, I had met a teacher through the personal ads in the local newspaper. She—Alicia—had responded to my ad. I was still living in my one room at the time. We'd talk for hours on end; must have talked for five hours each night. She lived on the southwest side of the city. She had a beautiful voice, and I really liked her character on the phone. Just as importantly, she liked me too.

So, sometime later, we were to meet in a public place. I had chosen to meet in the lobby of a large hotel in downtown. I went to the gift shop and purchased a beautiful plant, and brought along a small cooler filled with brie cheese with crackers, and grapes. I still remember when I asked to meet her, she told me it had to be in a public place and that she had my name and phone number on caller ID. Her brother was a policeman, and if he didn't hear from her within a half hour after we were scheduled to meet, he'd come looking for her—and me. I asked her if she wanted to see my driver's license. She thought that was very cute.

We had met on a Saturday, about 11:00 am. I was so nervous. I had parked my car in the parking garage below. I knew my way around the place because I had worked in the hotel at one time. While coming up in the elevator, I had the sudden urge to go to the bathroom. I learned later that I actually walked right past her, where she was sitting with some other women, so I wouldn't recognize her right away. But when I came back from the restroom, I walked up to her and asked her if she was Alicia.

She replied yes. I had found her! There were two people that I wanted to meet in life, that I hoped for as a partner. First was a medical person and the other was a teacher. I got really lucky this time around. The Lord had found me my life's partner.

We decided to walk to the beach for a short lunch break. I put the cheese with crackers and grapes in a cooler, and gave her the beautiful succulent plant. We talked for a long time.

I remember she was wearing a long-sleeve blue shirt with a white tank top underneath it, and as she leaned back, I could see her full breasts through her shirt. I liked full-figured women. She had dark brown, curly hair, and a beautiful face, cute nose, and awesome lips. I told myself that I was the luckiest guy in the world to have met such a beautiful woman. I was very attracted to her, and wanted her to be my girl.

We went on several more dates together. She was a vegetarian at the time, so I took her to a vegetarian restaurant. It was more of a surprise and she loved it.

I was still working with Brad at that time. He made working there feel like hell, because after three months, I still didn't get the raise he promised me. He should have never said he was going to give me one in the first place, if he couldn't deliver on his promise. In the beginning, I really thought he and I were going to be friends, but all he had on his mind was his newest girlfriend, whose father owned a huge company. He bragged to me that they had sex almost every night when they got together. Things had become even worse for me after I called the main office to complain about him. They then arranged a meeting with the both of us, the area supervisor, and the HR personnel director. I was really nervous, because there seemed to be so many people against me; I should have asked Alicia in the beginning to come with me for moral support and thought that maybe she could help me. But I was so stupid, and told her that I could do this on my own. She already knew that I was manic depressive because I told her on our second date. My sister in law told me if I didn't tell Alicia, she would tell her about my illness.

I didn't want anyone to know about my illness at my workplace. Alicia, however, would not let me go alone, but I really thought I could handle this on my own.

I went to the meeting, where I was made to look like a fool, and since Chef Brad was at the company for so many years, it made him look stronger and me look weaker. The personnel director didn't want Alicia to come in to the meeting, so I lost round one right off the bat. I'm not sure what happened next, but I asked the area supervisor, if he could write me a letter of recommendation, and he actually agreed. Oh, but I was transferred to a different location on the south side. By this time, I had moved in with Alicia and had given up my apartment.

Alicia and I were going to meet her aunt and uncle in a small town in Indiana to celebrate their 50th wedding anniversary. We were driving in her car, and we got to the tollway when the car broke down. Thankfully, I had a motor club membership, and so we called; it took about an hour before we got help, and when the guy found us, he wanted money for both tolls because he said he couldn't find us and drove through the tollway twice to get to our car.

During all this turmoil, Alicia said something so wonderful to me. She said that after we brought the car to the shop, and got home, that she wanted to make passionate love to me. Wow! I was feeling really special now. Well readers, we did just that—all afternoon!

I worked for the same company a few more months, and then I quit, no longer being in Chef Brad's grip. He definitely was a toxic person for me.

It seems like I make a lot of bad decisions about the people I think are my friends.

I was with Alicia for almost six months, and we fell in love with each other, so decided to get married. I didn't have a job, but was looking. I called my mother and told her about Alicia and that we were going to get married. Sometime earlier, I had told my mother about Alicia, saying I had found someone very special. But at that time, Alicia and I were still just talking on the phone, so my mother's response was, "Sure, you found someone," as she wasn't very convinced, due to my previous relationships. When she finally met Alicia, she loved her as much as I did and they became very close.

CHAPTER **FIVE**

Just today I went to the car wash and ended up waiting over three hours. There were a lot of people there, as it was a great day for a car wash. I had the urgency to talk to someone—anyone. I just couldn't control myself; I was feeling lonely, and helpless, and I didn't know why. I just urgently needed to talk to someone. This doesn't happen very often, but it sometimes can get in the way of meeting someone nice. Today, though, I met a man from Minnesota. He wore a Harley shirt, so I asked him where his Harley was. He said it was 400 miles away. I seldom meet real men that can be kind and friendly without being jerks. He made my day, as we talked a bit. I think he said he had served in the Navy. (Thank you for serving our country. God bless you, and be safe.)

I went to church for the first time in like five years; at a church in our community. I was a little saddened that the pastor wasn't there to preach. We were watching videos on large screens. I didn't stay long; left about an hour into it. It was pitch black outside; I didn't feel comfortable driving in the night anymore, and I had come alone, as Alicia wasn't feeling well. But I did pray for her, and my mama, that they would both get better. I felt as though I needed to go back to the church where I was baptized back Germany in 1991, at the Church of Latter Day Saints. There is a church of that faith close to my home.

———

Alicia was so nice to let me live with her on the south side of the city, where she had a one-bedroom apartment on the second floor of a small three-story building. She had been married before, but had never lived with anyone she wasn't married to. I guess she really loved me!

I remember it was the fall of 1998, and we were to meet Alicia's brother Rob, and his wife, Dottie. Rob was on the police force, and Dottie was a homemaker. We all met at Alicia's apartment for supper. Alicia had warned me that her brother wasn't very talkative, so don't be insulted if he didn't talk much. Alicia and Dottie left Rob and me alone while they went to find an ATM. Rob and I seemed to hit it off well; he was the quiet type, and me being the talkative type must of talked more than he did, but he was very nice. When the girls got back, they were actually surprised that the two of us got along so well. I have a brother, but Rob was different; someone I could look up to and respect.

Alicia and I were talking about love and marriage, so we set a date to get married. We had planned a big wedding and had reserved the date at a banquet hall. I was taking classes to convert to Catholicism, Alicia's religion. We had hoped to have children at that time and it was important to Alicia that our children be raised with religion. I was six weeks into convert classes when the priest and the deacon got into an argument and cancelled the classes. I'd have to start all over taking these classes.

Alicia had been married before and had a big wedding. She felt betrayed by the church when my convert classes were cancelled and didn't want to spend the next year or two saving for a big wedding. She just wanted me. She took a day off work and we got married at City Hall. Afterwards, we called everyone and told them we were married. It was January 27, 1999. I wasn't working at the time, and Alicia seemed to be okay with that then. I had filed disability papers for my asthma.

Living with Alicia in the apartment, I was experiencing a difficult time breathing because of the factories that were behind her place posed a threat for my fragile lungs. We moved from there after about six months to an area on the north side of the city. I remember that Mama paid for the moving costs for a moving company that we used on the south side. I also remember when Mama came with her husband to look at the apartment, and asked the landlord if the house had cockroaches, to which he replied no, not at all. That was our main concern with living there as the house was only two houses away from the river. Our place was spacious, with beautiful hardwood floors throughout, a large front room, large kitchen, two smaller bedrooms, a sunroom and a nice backyard. Alicia had a bit of a longer drive to work, but she didn't mind. Alicia was special education teacher. She loves her work, and especially the children, and getting involved with their parents. I know for a fact that my wife is a great teacher, because even the little ones, when they'd see her, would run up to her and ask for hugs. I had been at her school a few times and played with the children with their thinking games. At the end of the day, my wife would be exhausted, but happy.

It was our choice not to have children, but we do admire other parents who have such precious ones, and sometimes it makes us wish we would have decided to have children. Oh well.

Our downstairs neighbors caused us a lot of stress. It was nerve racking. We weren't there long when we knew we weren't going to get along, and had made a mistake of renting the place. Water bugs were popping up all around the house, and our landlord, had claimed that the house didn't have any. We shared the washing machine and dryer, which was in the basement, and which caused scheduling problems. We had a very small utility storage unit for our extra things. There was a grassy area behind the house that was covered in cat feces and smelled, from our downstairs neighbors' cat, instead of the nice back yard we thought we'd have.

Our area was arranged beautifully by my wife, Alicia. She had exceptional taste, and knew just how the furniture should be arranged. We had an open house party for our family and friends. Dealing with the neighbors and the cat got to be too much for both of us.

After that, we moved into the nice two-bedroom apartment a bit further north. The street we were on was a one-way street. Living on the second floor of a three-story building, I felt a bit uneasy because other people lived above us, and there would be sounds from above and below. And one never knew how bad different neighbors would be. This wasn't too bad though, as we stayed there for about four years.

A lot happened in those four years.

My mother was entering her twenty-fourth year on the radio. I was talking to my brother Peter, who had been married his second wife, Bonnie, for several years. They never had children, but Peter had Daniella, with his first wife, Diane. For some reason, I don't think Peter wanted me to know where Daniella was living, so in April of 2000, on my mother's birthday—which is also Daniella's birthday—when my wife and I decided we wanted to give Daniella a gift for her birthday, we asked Peter if he would give her a package for her birthday.. He was fine with the idea, so we gave the wrapped gift to Peter. But we outsmarted him, as we put our address and phone number in the gift with a note that we were trying to get in touch with her for some time, and asked that she contact us when she had a chance. It turned out that Daniella lived four blocks from us. Peter had lied and told her I was working in Europe and told me that she was "not worth (my) time". He said that about his own daughter! What a lying bastard.

I was seeing a doctor for my manic depression, was on disability, and had applied for handicap parking, but had to wait for about a year to get a space by the front entrance of our building.

There was a couple who lived directly below us with two young teenagers. We got into an argument one Saturday morning because I brought my laundry down quite early. She started yelling at me that she had been doing laundry for ten years early on Saturday mornings, and that I messed up her plans for the day. Her son, who was quite big—bigger than me—got involved. He became quite angry because I had said something negative to his mother, and told me that nobody treats his mother like that. I said that I was there first and he said his mother was. I told them, no problem, go ahead and do their laundry. That was my first negative encounter with them. They were difficult to deal with on a daily basis.

We tried to be good renters. When I was late with mailing the first rent check, I drove all the way to our landlord's home to give him the check so it would be on time.

Alicia and I liked the area, but the airplanes coming in and out were such a hindrance. Noise from neighbors, airplanes, traffic enraged me and made me irritable.

Alicia was still working as a teacher; I was on my

second year of collecting disability and was not working. I kept our home in order and cooked dinner to be ready when Alicia came home.

I remember going to the 2000 Auto Show with Peter, and found a really cool car. It was very air dynamic and was big enough for me to get into. I'm six-foot-three and weigh about 300 pounds. The car was perfect. So when I got home, I convinced Alicia that we should look at this car, and went to a dealership, test-drove it, and bought it, with a three-year warranty. Midnight black with a standard shift, very nice interior, and decent fuel mileage. Alicia trusted my judgement about buying this car, even though I'm not so sure she should have.

The first year we had the new car we had about 11 recalls. From the front windshield needing replacement, to other replacements. I drove a loaner car quite a bit, that I got from the dealer when we brought it in.

Daniella finally contacted us. We learned that she only lived a few blocks from where we were currently living. We set a time to meet with her on that Saturday, at a restaurant close to both of us. Alicia, although she was meeting her for the first time, talked to her the most. We were there a long time and made plans to meet up again, and this time she would bring my nephew, her 3 year old son. Daniella had grown up to be very pretty and sweet; she reminded me of pictures I had seen of my mother as a young child, and Daniella's face had a resemblance to her.

I don't remember where we met again. It was summertime, and I think we took them to the beach which is always worth the trip, in spite of the lack of parking spots. We had to pay five dollars each to get to the beach and we always paid for Daniella and her son. Since the sun was so hot, we made sure that we all had on plenty of sunscreen. They had lifeguards on duty, which was good. Since the sun felt very hot, we only stayed a few hours, as we didn't want to get sunburned. We decided to stop at a McDonald's for a bite to eat. We then took Daniella and her son home, dropped them off, and went back to our home.

After that, Daniella would often stop by with her son, which was nice, so we could see them often. She would call after work almost every night and ask what we were doing for dinner. Alicia would always tell her we had plenty of food, so bring her son and come have dinner with us. It became our daily routine and we loved it. One day when they were over, I made these terrific crepes with strawberry jam; Daniella loved them, and it became her favorite sweet dish that I made for her. I liked them just as much; they are even better made with whole wheat flour. We spent a lot of time together, and yes, we talked about Peter and how badly he had treated Daniella growing up. He never paid child support, she didn't even have his phone number. She'd have to call my father, her grandfather, to get a message to Peter; and then he would call Daniella.

So this went on for about a year.

At one point, I had told Peter that we knew where Daniella lived. I think he was angry at that, but there was nothing he could do about it. I had mentioned this to mama, and she then wanted to see Daniella and her great grandson, whom she had never met!

———

Mama is always very busy. She has that German radio show every week that she has been on since the early 70's. She was the host of the show and wrote the show, commercials, did the billing, advertising, everything The commercials for the show were hard to do, especially in German. At one point, when I was living with Mama in 1995, I asked her if she would teach me how to talk on the radio. We did a mock trial and she said I did a horrible job, as I was breathing into the microphone before I would start talking. Mama didn't believe I had what it took to be good on radio, which made me feel really sad, since I was her son. Her own husband had a great voice, but was terrible at the mechanics of the radio board, which Mama said only she could do. Hey, we all have to start somewhere. I kept asking her to teach me, but my asthma made it impossible for me.

I might have been able to do it, but Mama was too skeptical of me. I felt like she was playing my father's role, of you can't do it because you're not good enough. I had heard that a hundred times from my father, so I didn't need to hear it from her, too.

Well, I never did get to be on the radio because Mama didn't believe in me. I really thought that with a little training, I could do a great job. After all, I am a hard worker, and I knew I could do it. I thought that practice, practice, and more practice would make it perfect, but Mama wasn't convinced. So that was the end of that.

My wife is worried that I may have a manic episode if I write too much and don't rest enough between writing. So far, I haven't felt that I might.

In was February of 2003, and we had the new car for almost three years, and weren't happy with it. Stuff happens, and we made a stupid choice. Alicia and I took the car to a used car dealer to see how much we could get for it. It was after the warranty, and they wanted almost a thousand dollars to take the car from us. This was not one of my better moves. The timing was good though, as we had just gotten our tax return money, and so we paid them the money to take our car so we could reduce our monthly payments.. We still owed $8,000 on the car. They must have been laughing all the way to the bank, and thought that we really must have been a couple fools. Again, Alicia trusted I knew what I was doing.

We only had the one car, and then we made another poor money decision. I believe it was in July of 2003, when we went to look at another vehicle. We were in the showroom and saw this beautiful SUV, it was a beauty. One of the salesmen came up to us and asked how much we could afford. Yeah, stupid answer on our part; we must have had suckers written all over our faces. We ended up buying the new vehicle and having more debt than before. At least the rent was cheaper than the monthly payment on our new four-wheel drive SUV.

I believe it was in the year 2000, that we got a Lovebird as a pet from my father, who was then a Lovebird breeder. This was my first Lovebird, and we decided on the name Booboo. We weren't supposed to have pets in the building, but kept it anyway. Booboo was so cute, with his green and turquoise blue colors. One of my therapists thought it was a great idea to have a pet; pet therapy was great. He was very quiet and didn't chirp that much, but he was a hand-fed Lovebird. He'd get by your ears and put one foot on the lower part of your earlobe, and his beak in your ear. We got another Lovebird in 2006, and named him Stormy. He was the same color as Booboo, and even though, he too, was a hand-feed Lovebird, he was a little wild at times. To our disappointment, we lost both of them. Booboo in April of 2014, and Stormy in April of 2015. I missed them both so much, as they were like our children, our beloved pets. I had buried them on the property near where we live. I wrote letters to them both and put them in Ziploc bags with flowers and buried those with them. Booboo and Stormy are greatly missed.

My tears are running down my eyes as I write this.

I will never forget these small pets that gave such big joy to both of us. God bless them.

The time that we lived close to Daniella went quite fast. When I got into an argument with Peter and told him he didn't deserve a daughter like Daniella, she got angry with me for bringing her name into the argument and quit talking to me and Alicia.

In April of 2004, we bought our first condo in the northwest suburbs, on the third floor with nobody living above us. We had a pool that was open in the summer; there was like a large lake in the middle of the condos, and a tennis court. It was beautiful here, and reminded me of when I had been to Wisconsin. I was so happy to have a place to call our own. Our condo was a two-bedroom, two bath, and our unit faced the lake and the other condos on the west side of the property. Alicia had a long drive to work, though, from home; over an hour one way. She loved where she worked and she loved where we lived, so she didn't mind the drive at first.

By this time, I had seen about ten therapists and they all were just plain bad. I wasn't comfortable with any of them. I was still on disability, but had worked part time as a security guard driving a mobile unit, checking for suspicious activity around the mall. Sometimes I had to walk in the inside of the mall and make the rounds. Then I worked for another security company close to home, around 2005.

I still had a lot of problems with my bipolar illness between working and being at home.

Sometimes, I'd be so nervous about waking up on time, I didn't sleep all night. Sometimes, the stress of the job was unbearable. I wanted to work and help support my home, but as hard as I tried, I was getting sicker and more stressed. Alicia told me the extra money wasn't worth it because it caused me so much stress.

My father, having always been a selfish person, and making me believe I had never been good enough, to whom I brought something to his attention thinking he would be very proud of me, instead, would give me a kick in the behind. I told him that I was going to write a great book someday. He said laughing, "Yeah? And who's going to read it?" I was so hurt and disheartened. When I got home, I started punching myself in the face as if to do the work of my father like he'd do to me so long ago. I felt terrible at the same time, because I really hurt, both emotionally and physically.

I have been punching myself for years now, and Alicia is afraid I will have some sort of dementia, like my mother.

I remember that when 2006 came, Alicia and I were fighting about something; I'm not sure what it was, but my behavior had changed dramatically. I was having a flight of ideas; my mind knew what it wanted to do, but I was fighting with myself. I was off my medication for a while now; maybe a week or more. My plan was to go to Germany to escape the pain.

Alicia just told me I took a box of watches, a video camera, all of our credit cards, and my passport. She said I was so irritable, that my Aunt Christine had planned for me to come there, and had told Tanya that I was leaving my wife to come to Germany to be with her instead. Along with that, my so called "friend", Matt, was encouraging me to go. He had me open a credit card and send the bill to his house so Alicia wouldn't know. I was going to use the card to pay for my trip. What I didn't know was that Matt wanted me out of the picture so he could have my wife!

Alicia's uncle died the night of Thanksgiving, and my timing couldn't have been worse, as Alicia was on the verge of a severe breakdown with all the stress of me, her uncle's death (he and her aunt had raised her and her brothers when her mother left her).

I left the house and took the car to the other side of the lake, threw my car keys in the trunk, and left to go to the nearby hotel that was about a quarter mile down the road. I remember asking for a taxi to go to a local restaurant. I was making it difficult for someone to follow my tracks, and was very paranoid that someone was following me. When I got to the restaurant, I drank a lot of beer in an hour. I remember that I stood up with my suitcase and started to walk toward the highway that led to the airport. I was walking on the right side of the highway, and was nervous that a vehicle would hit me, so I moved to the far right near the grassy area. It took me about an hour to walk to the airport. Matt had planned this trip with me; he lived on the property and said he would meet up with me in Germany. With me going to Germany, he thought Alicia would be available to him.

When I got to the airport, I was so tired; my legs had really taken a beating. I proceeded to the terminal where my plane comes in and out. I booked a flight for a round-trip ticket, as it was less expensive than a one-way flight. I said that my grandmother died, and they gave me 30 percent off the charge of the flight. I remember requesting a wheelchair, and they complied.

Meanwhile, while I was traveling to Germany, Alicia called the police when she couldn't find me. She reported I was bipolar and off my medication. Due to the fact that I was mentally ill, they sent two detectives to our home. Alicia later told me that they looked through the desktop computer for information as to where I was going. By that time I was on a plane. I had planned on visiting my grandmother. The flight was about eight and a half hours. I had not slept since leaving home, even though the walk to the airport tired me. I was so mixed with mania, and my mind had a flight of ideas, trying to tell me what to do. When the plane had taxied into the terminal, people who were handicapped were the first ones to leave the plane. Since there was a wheelchair waiting for me, I was one of the first who left the plane. The attendant would then hurry one through customs, and as for me, since I was a German-born immigrant, they waved me right through as they said: "Willkommen nach Deutschland" which means Welcome to Germany. I felt as if I was home again, and found my mind racing.

I began to have sleeping problems; I spent the first night in a hotel. I just couldn't seem to fall asleep, especially since I had no medication with me. When the next day came, I got up early, and called Christine and told her that I was in Germany. She said "Good." I told her that I was going to visit my grandmother first. To be sure that my grandmother was home, I called her first. She did not pick up, and I thought that maybe she didn't hear the phone ring. So I took a taxi to her apartment, and while the taxi driver was waiting for me, I went to ring her doorbell several times. Still no answer. I was quite sad that I didn't get to see her, so went back into the taxi and took it to the train station, so I could take the train to see Tanya. My mind was still racing; and thought that I was making stupid mistakes. I called Tanya from the train station and told her that the train wouldn't be there until late, around nine p.m. It was about 80 miles, but the train made several stops, which would make it take longer.

Then, I was so confused. I got off the train too early at another stop just before Bielefeld. Then it would take another 40 minutes to get there by train, putting me closer to 10:00 pm to pull into the main train station. I was standing on the train platform and did not see Tanya. I became quite nervous, thinking that she was not coming to get me, and started to panic. I was going to lose it right then and there. I began to sweat very heavily, and was so turned around and confused, I almost forgot where I was. I walked over to where all the taxis were parked, because I didn't see Tanya anywhere. Then, when I was about to give up, I saw her driving around the train station. I held my hands up to motion to her that I made it, hoping she'd see me. She parked her car and we ran to each other and hugged one another. She told me that she thought I had changed my mind about coming. She told me how excited she was when Aunt Christine had shared the wonderful news that I was coming to Germany.

We then drove to her apartment that she shared with a roommate. I don't remember the roommate's name, but

I did know that she was going to school with Tanya at that time. Tanya told me she had to be in school very early in the morning and that she was going to bed, and that there was a place to sleep on the couch, already made up for me. The only problem was I was too long for the couch, but I decided I would sleep the best I could there. Tanya had said that if I was hungry that there was food for me in the fridge to snack on, and she had a few bottles of mineral water there on the dining room table for me to drink. She told me to wait until she got home from school the next day, and that we would celebrate then.

I had a difficult time falling asleep, with no medication for several weeks. I didn't know how I was going to survive without the proper medication. When I woke up the next morning, I discovered I was the only one home; Tanya and her roommate had already left. I looked at the clothing I still had on from travelling. I had given away all the watches and the video camera to the attendants who had pushed me in the wheelchair at the airport.

For a few moments, I felt sad and lonely, and was thinking about Alicia and what I had done. My flight of ideas had gotten me into so much trouble. I knew my parents were probably scared. I was thinking about the Lovebirds, especially Booboo and how that tiny thing had missed me. What had I done? I really messed up with my wife, Alicia. I started to miss her terribly. But I was in Germany. Alicia would probably never forgive me.

Is this what I really wanted to do, or was the mania just taking over?

I then called Aunt Christine, and she seemed to be

pleased that I came back to Germany. It was about 7 a.m., and I knew she would be up by then, drinking her coffee, like she did when I was living with her. She told me later that she was about to lose it because they didn't know where I was. I stayed in the apartment all morning, but knew that I had to go back home to my Alicia. Then I left the apartment and took a taxi that I waved down, to the train station where I booked a train to Aunt Christine's house..

I was about 500 miles away, when my mania was taking over, and I couldn't think anymore. I was so stressed, had a bad headache, and the train trip to Aunt Christine's would take about eight hours. The train made frequent stops on its way. On the trip, I was in great physical and emotional pain. I felt so guilty about what I had done to Alicia, that I began to hurt myself again. I went to the restroom so no one else could see me, and beat the crap out of myself. When I returned to my seat in the train, everyone glared at me, with quizzical looks. I buried my face in my sweater, so no one could see me. I was getting chest pains, and a total sadness overcame me.

What had I done?

I wished that I was home with Alicia instead of going to Aunt Christine's. I knew that I was not being normal. When I finally made it to the main train station, I called Aunt Christine and asked if Uncle Ray could come pick me up. She said he'd be there in a half hour, so I had some time to kill. There was an internet café next to the train station, so I went there, got on my account in the U.S. and saw that Alicia was trying to get in touch with me by email! She said I should call or write and that we could work this out, that I should just come home.

I felt so relieved that she had contacted me. I can't remember what I did at that moment, but I had to get to the area where cars come pick one up. As soon as I got there, I saw Uncle Ray was there. We got to their home in less than 20 minutes. I went into the old house, and there in the kitchen was Aunt Christine. She gave me a big hug and welcome. I was a bit happy then; it had been almost four days of travel. She asked me if Tanya knew I was there, and I said not really. She told me I should call her right away and let her know where I was. So I did. Tanya didn't know why I had left her apartment, and was looking for me. I said I was very sorry, but I had to see Aunt Christine, and just took off.

Somehow, arrangements were made for me to go back to Alicia. Aunt Christine had talked to Alicia and Alicia knew her plan to reunite me with Tanya and destroy our marriage. Alicia told her to burn in hell for trying to destroy our marriage. See, Aunt Christine had planned for me to leave Alicia and go back to Tanya. My aunt had never met Alicia, so she couldn't have anything against her. My aunt was friends with Tanya and wanted me to be with her, not Alicia. I was sick and let myself be manipulated. Again.

I took the train to the airport, and then took a plane back home. It was a nine-hour flight. When I got to there I passed through customs; they knew my name and asked if I was he, and when I said yes, I was told that the customs agents were waiting for me. I didn't know what they were talking about, but as I passed through the gate, I saw Alicia, my father, and my mother. They all gave me big hugs and said that they had missed me.

Alicia drove me to a hospital immediately. I had been almost a full seven days in Germany and several weeks before without medication. It felt like my brain was fried, and I was totally exhausted and dehydrated. I was given a new doctor at this facility. When I met him, I told him I thought he was the devil and that he scared me. I would be staying there a while, and knew I wasn't going to get out as easily as I thought I could. But at least I was going to get some medication for my head. The facility was a closed unit. I remember being there, but I do not remember how long, nor having any group therapy classes. I needed a few days to adjust to the new medications that they were giving me.

I do remember one woman who was there in the same unit as I. Her name was Pam, and for some reason, we were drawn to each other psychically, not physically or emotionally. There were a lot of people in this unit who heard voices in their heads, but I wasn't one of them. Pam and I thought we had something in common. I had mentioned to her that I felt the Lord's presence; she said she felt the same way. We both believed that God was going to send a spaceship down to earth and pick up all the sick people and take us to heaven. I really wanted to believe that. But I know it wasn't really true. I was here for a few weeks. I was glad that Alicia came to visit as often as she could.

Finally, it was time to go home. The doctor had put

me on new medication, and I was to see him every week, until he believed that I was in a good place.

So 2006 had been a bad year for me—emotionally—and for Alicia, too. Two years went by and then the same thing happened to me again, but this time I was on my medications. I went to Germany after a major fight with Alicia, and I still remember that when we were in the air, I had asked the flight attendant what the numbers on the tail were. She said she would ask the captain for me. When it was announced that we were going to make and emergency landing, I knew there was something wrong. The flight attendant must have told the captain that I was mentally ill and that we needed to land as soon as possible. When we landed, I was taken off the plane by police. Everyone stared at me like I was a criminal, and who caused the flight to divert.

The airport doctor checked me out. The plane didn't wait for me, but continued to Germany without me. In London they let me go, after they determined I wasn't a threat to anyone but myself. I took the next plane I could get on to Germany, and from there I took a train 800 miles traveling for 18 hours.

I called Aunt Christine from the phone on the train; she was happy to hear my voice, and tried to calm me, as I was having a difficult time, even on the medication. Once I arrived in at her home, I felt much better, because things were familiar. I had lived there in 1983 to 1986 when I was going to chef school in Munich.

While there, I must have talked to Alicia on the phone. She knew I was unstable again, and said that when I'd go back home, I'd have to go to yet another mental hospital. I think I was in Germany less than a week, before I returned to the United States, and just like the other time, Alicia took me to a hospital. This time, my passport was about to expire and if I didn't leave Europe soon, I'd be stuck there!

The mental health hospital was next to the main hospital. This time, the doctor tried to adjust my medication and put me on Lithium tablets, and for some reason gave me too much medication. One day, when Alicia came to visit and asked a nurse what was wrong with me, the nurse replied that I was just fine. Alicia told her I looked like I was a walking stroke victim. They kept telling her I was fine. The next day, they realized that I had Lithium poisoning, and had to do what's called a med wash and clean all the medication from my system. Lithium can be a great medication, but has to be monitored very closely. Even on high doses of lithium, I was still experiencing mania. The lithium wasn't working for me.

I had a lot of good therapy there, including art therapy in which I drew a unique picture of my feelings while in the hospital, and when I got out, Alicia had it framed. I am hoping it will make the cover of this book when it is finished. We'll see.

When I was at the hospital, I kept asking if my sister-in-law, Bonnie, worked at the main hospital as an intensive care nurse, and many people knew her. I somehow felt a bit relieved because a family member worked there. Not that Bonnie would ever visit or even admit to being related to me. Peter forbid her to have contact with me.

I finally got out of the hospital and went home with Alicia. I was so happy to be home again, and that this ordeal was behind me. Once again, I had really let every down who meant anything in my life.

I'm thankful that I had people who love me: Alicia, Rob, Dottie, mama, Alter, and a few others.

———

It is important to have a good social safety net with friends and family members, who can recognize potential depression triggers like the feeling of hopelessness, feeling like you're not good enough, loss of interest in things, feeling sad, loss of a job or someone, suicidal thoughts, and not taking medication. I've had all those thoughts before, but just telling someone else your feelings helps tremendously, or going to the hospital emergency room, or calling 911. Otherwise, it can lead to trying to kill oneself over these feelings and stupid ideas.

I had to fail, to go through all this to get where I am. Remember that you're not alone in the world, that there are people who care about you and who love you. You may think you are alone, but you are not. I care about what happens to you. I give a damn about you. I may not know all the answers, but I've been through a lot of grief and sorrow, and if I can't help you, I'll find someone who can help you. You're not alone.

I wanted to write this book for over 25 years. I would tell people that and never went through with it until now.

I've had so many near-death experience, and the Almighty God kept me around long enough to finally get this done; to write to you, the reader.

My roller coaster ride didn't end yet. I had one more near-death experience, in 2011. My wife knows more about this horrible scare than me, because I was unconscious most of the time, so she has written the last chapter of this book to tell you about it.

I had TTP (Thrombotic Thrombocytopenic Purpura) which is a rare blood disorder where blood clots form in small blood vessels throughout the body. The clots can limit or block the flow of oxygen-rich blood to the body's organs such as the brain, kidneys, and heart.

We had been buying unpasteurized dairy from a farmer in hopes of getting "healthy". I loved to eat steak tartare, which is raw hamburger. We don't really know what caused me to get sick, but those were two potential triggers. I'll never how just how I got this blood disorder; all I know is that I had become ill in 2011. My wife will explain more later.

———

It was March, 2016. I went to visit my mother and felt profound sadness for her, as her disease had reduced her to the mind of a small child.

Damn the disease.

She used to be on the top of her game; she had success,

meaning, and purpose. The Lewy Body Dementia had taken all that from her. She's in good hands now; we found a memory care facility for her just 20 minutes away. She's even found love again, which is remarkable at her age of 82. I'm so proud of my mother; she really had a great life, especially with her 31 years on the German radio show. She was the voice to listen to on Saturdays.

Just after my TTP illness, I obtained a part time job with a security camera company in a nearby town. How I got the job was that we had to do contract work on our property, and Gregg was here analyzing the work that needed to be done. When I asked him if his company was hiring, he said that Don does the hiring, and that I should talk to him about getting a job with the company. I then met Don, and soon got a job as a telemarketer for the company.

Several months had passed and the security camera company I was working for moved to a larger office, and added more personnel, including two secretaries, and more salespersons. I was pretty much doing everything for the company in addition to making phone calls. I cleaned the restroom, took out the garbage, made coffee, and did pickup and deliveries. I had a small car so I couldn't pick up much, but would pick up lunch. I really liked it there. At one point I was promised a job as a warehouse manager, which never came to be, because Gregg and I had our differences. He didn't want to talk to me first thing in the morning because my bipolar chatting would seem to tick him off; just talking to him seemed to stress him out. I got along with Don, but he was usually too busy to chat as he was always on his cellphone. The company trusted me with a credit card, which I never abused, unlike some of the other workers who would use their card for personal things such as gas, cigarettes, and lunch.

I told my wife Alicia, that the people at the company had started treating me differently when she asked why I was so upset when I had come home from work. So I wrote a letter to Don and Gregg explaining why I had decided to quit after being there for almost two years; that I had finally had enough of them. Both guys were younger than me by 25 years. Don was the CEO, and Gregg the President of the company.

Previously, I had had an accident at a nail salon (September of 2013), which was very traumatizing and painful. I had fallen and could not work anymore at the company. When II

I ended up having to retain a lawyer because the nail salon was very negligent. I remember that about a year after my accident, I asked Don for my job back and he said Gregg didn't want me to work for them ever again, saying I was not to be trusted. Don had only been stringing me along, making it seem he was really interested in having me come back, but when it came right down to it, he said Gregg was the one who didn't want me back. What a jerk! Another toxic person in my life.

———

Then there is the story about Paul, an executive chef. I helped open a famous restaurant in a hotel with other cooks in 1987. I remember that he was a bastard, the meanest chef I had ever met or worked with. I worked there for two years, and busted my butt to please the guy, but he didn't care. I was a line cook for the restaurant, which had a French theme.

There was this time when a few chefs from various hotels from various cities in Germany were invited to cook for us at the best restaurant in town. Chef Paul had expected me to work on my days off to accommodate these chefs because I spoke German. One chef in particular, Peter got along quite well with me, and even asked me if I wanted to come to his hotel in Germany and work for him. I felt so honored, and of course said yes. I remember that Chef Paul was so angry with me for saying I'd take the job in Germany, that he called me nasty names and threw pots and pans at me. I went to the Human Resources department to complain, but they wouldn't do anything about the situation. Then one day when I was making soup for lunch service at the restaurant, he came and tasted my soup, then took the pot and poured the entire stock pot of potato soup into the sink and instructed me to start over. That was it! No more abuse. I quit that day and walked out.

Then my friend Alter got me the job at a major airline as a chef for the wide-body kitchens on the airfield of a huge airport. I really liked my job there. I had great peers and I was finally making some good money. But there was one problem—the deadline for me to accept the job in Germany was approaching, and I really didn't want to go at this point, but my father was pressuring me to go and to give up the job at the airlines, and so I took the job even though I really didn't want to leave. I guess I was still trying to please my father.

It was September of 1990, and I was really sad about leaving, but then thought that this might be a positive move for me. I got the position as Commis de Cuisine and worked in the Entremetre, which meant the soup and vegetable station; on the line again, as this was a very fast-paced kitchen. Chef Peter,was the expediter for the kitchen. I remember I was making seven to ten pounds of spätzle on a daily basis. That was a lot of work; I had to work hard and earned very little in this hotel. It's all about the name—working for the hotel, as when you finished your time there, other hotels would look at you and realize that since you worked in one of the best hotels, that you knew your profession very well.

At first I slept upstairs in one of the hotel rooms, and shared the room with a guy from Italy. He was rarely there, so I pretty much had the room to myself, which I was quite happy about, as I am so sensitive to noises when I sleep. Someone snoring can bother me. Of course, the downside of living in the hotel is that you're always on call to work.

A few months later, I moved to a small town, which was about 40 miles west of where I worked and I rented a two-bedroom apartment, in what ended up being the poorest section of town. On the upside, my favorite grocery store was within walking distance. This town was also the birthplace of my mother's husband.

One day I met Frieda, an elderly woman, when I was standing in line with my produce in my arms, when she asked me if I wanted to step in front of her in line, to which I replied no, that I was off work that day and had plenty of time. She was a sweet woman, probably in her 70's. We started walking off in the same direction, and then when I turned to go in the direction I lived, she wished me a good day and said that she hoped that we would meet again. Frau K. invited me to her apartment for lunch one day. We had a great time, and later became good friends. She liked to cook for me on my days off, even though I was a cook. Her husband, Paul, had died a few years before. A good friend of hers, and her daughter, both thought that I might have an ulterior motive, being friends with this elderly woman, but I assured them that that was not my intention, that we were just friends. One day I became ill, and she brought me homemade chicken soup. I was so happy that someone would take care of me like that, so far away from home, where it was difficult to find good friends, as people weren't too trusting because of the war of 1945. Frau K. even gave me money so I could fly home to see my family that summer. I was only earning about $1500 a month, which didn't quite leave me enough money to purchase a plane ticket home.

I needed to see my friends and family back in America, so went on vacation for a few weeks and then returned to my job in Germany. Upon my return, I had a meeting with the director of the hotel, who told me that my work performance was so poor that they had to let me go. I just knew it was because of me being bipolar, and couldn't figure out what I had done that was so bad that they had to fire me. I was so angry that my father had pressured me to take this job, even though I was doing well at the airline in America. So I told Frau K. what had happened, and that I was going to return to the States, and she said she would miss me, that I was a nice friend, and that we could write to each other.

Before going back to America, I had met these missionaries from the Church of Latter Day Saints, and got so involved with them that I agreed to be baptized at the state conference in the summer of 1989.

I was going back to America after being in Germany for about a year. My father was angry with me because I couldn't fulfill my duties as a chef at the hotel. I don't think my father knew that I suffered from bipolar illness. He just thought that I was a failure, which didn't help.

A few months had passed, when I received a letter from Frau K's daughter, giving me some very bad news— she had passed away from stomach cancer. I felt so sad; she was an extraordinary human being, and I had lost a great friend.

CHAPTER **SIX**

I remember that I was looking for a new job in about 1991, and found a position with a small catering company. There were less than 25 employees, and I really enjoyed working there. After a year, they made me head party chef and gave me the catering steward position. I was dating a girl named Carla, whom I had met at restaurant. It was a 70's bar, and she was there with her sister, another friend, and Bart, who was a friend of mine.

Somehow, Tanya got in touch with me and wanted to visit me. She did, and I broke up with Carla in that summer of 1991 .Tanya would go to the beach in Evanston to enjoy the sun while I went to work. She wanted me to move back to Germany with her, and move into her dorm at her school. We were in love and so that's what I did, and that's how I ended up there—in the dorm.

Tanya had known me through much of my childhood

life. I would go to Germany as a child and into my teens every year in the summer, usually in July. My grandfather and her father had worked at the same company and were neighbors.

The catering company didn't want to lose me as an employee because they really wanted me to advance. I felt the same way, but Tanya insisted I get a different job at one of the finer hotels in Germany.

My parents were shocked that I wanted to move to Germany again. My mother was still quite busy with her radio show. I remember there was a heavy metal music show after her show and I enjoyed listening to both shows.. I wish she would have taught me more about the radio business, as I would have definitely wanted to take over her show one day. But in 1991, I went back to Germany.

It makes me sad to think of it, because a year earlier I was there and didn't finish out the year at the hotel. I was there about two months, when I really got sick with asthma. I had been talking to my doctor and people who were rude and narcissistic. I shouldn't have opened the door for those people; I should have shut them down before they caused havoc in my life.

The other day, my father called and said he needed water, and wanted me to buy him some. I resent the way he says things to me. He never asked me to do anything. He told me what he wanted and expected me to fulfill his needs and wants.

A few months ago, when I was at his house, he told me that when he died, about all the things that I would get from him—the condo, a savings account, and so on. I asked if he was dying. He said, no, that he just wanted me to know. Now, if that isn't pressure on me, what is it? So, because I'll get this stuff later, I have to cater to you now? I should have kicked his ass; he had no respect at all for me as an adult. I must have sucker written all over my face.

In the end, my father was a hero; a man who had saved my grandmother, and my aunt during WWII. He had been walking for seven days on frozen ground. He was pulling a sled, with them on it, to safety. My father was a man before he was even 10 years old. I wish that I had known him better. He is now facing a large hurdle with uncertainty—at 84, he's on dialysis every 36 hours, and his momentum is slow and difficult. He has lost 70 percent of his eyesight. I can feel his pain, as he's nearing the end of his life., and I am saddened that he does not believe in our great God, to whom he once prayed to as a child. Maybe as he gets closer to the end, he will take the Lord as his Savior.

Oh Lord, please take my father to Heaven, he's been through so much. I was talking with him recently and he started to cry. I have not seen this side of my father before. I, who have been afraid of him for so long, finally have so much respect for him. He's my father, a great man. This book was written with the whole truth, nothing but the truth. So help me, God

He died in hospice in on December 21, 2016.

I was very fortunate to have spent the last three months with him, taking him to dialysis three days a week. He told me he wasn't afraid to die and that there was nothing waiting after you die. You just go in the ground. Period. I believe he was wrong, that he's with the Lord now, and with his mother, whom he so deeply missed.

CHAPTER **SEVEN**

THE STORY OF TTP

Max had become very tired, and was sleeping a lot. He was more lethargic than usual, but not depressed. Over our years of marriage, Max had been sick for most of them, but this was different. Valentine's Day 2011 was spent in the ER of our local hospital running tests because he was so ill, as well as 2 prior visits to the ER. They determined that he was dehydrated, gave him some fluids, and sent us home. He didn't get any better over the next week. I pumped him full of vitamins to help his energy, so when he told me his urine was very dark, I passed it off to the huge amount of supplements he was taking. Then he began bleeding from the rectum.

Several weeks prior to this, he was in the ER for a ruptured hemorrhoid, so I figured it had ruptured again. I was able to make logic out of everything that was happening. I was so tired! At this point, I did not know I was suffering from an autoimmune disease myself. Monday, February 21, I came home from work to find Max had slept all day. I was kind of upset, since I had worked all day, while he just slept. I just wanted to lay down and sleep! I asked Max what was for dinner, and he said, "I don't know. I'm so confused." That made me more angry, because the least he could do was to have dinner ready for us! I called our doctor who advised me to take him back to the ER because maybe he'd become dehydrated again. Damn, I just wanted to sleep.

We got dressed and went to the ER about six p.m. I gave the medical staff all his symptoms: dark urine, rectal bleeding, sleeping, confusion. They ran lots of tests and were going to admit him to the hospital. Exhausted, I left the ER at midnight while Max waited for a room.

The next morning, I called in sick to work and went to the hospital. They told me he was on the second floor, so I took the elevator up. When I got off the elevator, the sign said "Dialysis Floor," so I figured they didn't have a room anywhere else and put him there temporarily.

When I walked into Max's room, he was resting. He had developed a tremor in his hand. He was more con-fused than the previous day, but he recognized me. I was told by his doctor that Max was in end stage kidney failure and would need dialysis. What? Dialysis??? No, he was just dehydrated. It wasn't real to me. Was my husband going to die? They didn't know. How could this be happening? So many thoughts went through my mind. Doctors were asking me lots of questions. Does he eat hamburgers? From where? What restaurant, or grocery store?

At this point in our health journey we became part of a cow share program that enabled us to purchase raw, unpasteurized dairy. Right before Max got sick, I heard the story of State Police who stopped a raw dairy farmer and poured out all of his milk saying selling raw milk was illegal. I didn't tell the doctors we were drinking raw dairy because I didn't want the farmer to get in trouble!

The first thing I remember doing was calling my principal and telling her I would be out the rest of the week, that my husband could be dying. She was so kind and understanding, it made me cry even more. Over the next couple of days, Max got worse. He couldn't remember our home phone number to call me, he didn't know his mother's name, but he remembered his father's name perfectly. He couldn't even put on his own sleep apnea mask because the tremor was so bad. I wrote our phone number on the whiteboard next to his bed, but he couldn't dial the number. I was so afraid!

Thursday, February 24, was Max's first dialysis appointment. I spent the day with him and left when he was going to dialysis. I was told that most patients sleep during this procedure. I kissed him goodbye and told him I was tired, so I would see him the next day. He was barely aware of my presence, but he held me tightly. I went home and ordered pizza, my favorite comfort food at the time. I felt better after eating and resting, and thought I would surprise Max and go back to the hospital that evening when he finished dialysis. Before I even had the chance to get up from dinner, the phone rang. It was the hospital. Max had a seizure during dialysis and I needed to get to the hospital ASAP.

Luckily, the hospital is less than ten minutes from home. I got to the second floor and was greeted by Max's mother and his primary care doctor. The doctor said she was just about to leave for the day when she saw there was a code red in dialysis and knew it was Max, so she turned back to care for him. During dialysis, Max had a seizure and chewed his lips to pieces. I remember a blonde in a white coat asking for my signature; Max was being moved to the ICU. She said he had a rare autoimmune disease, TTP, that could be fatal. I remember walking with the doctor and my mother-in-law down long hallways to the ICU. I was so afraid!

Thrombotic thrombocytopenic purpura (TTP) is an extremely rare disease, with just 3.7 cases per year per million persons. The death rate from TTP is down to 10% or 20%. Before the use of plasmapheresis, the death rate was 90%.

When we finally got to Max's room in the ICU, he was a sight! His lips were chewed raw from the seizure. His chest was heaving as if he was struggling to breathe. I know there were alot of doctors, nurses, and assistants talking, but I don't remember anything. Except going in his room to help Max. I put his sleep apnea mask on him so he could breathe. I walked out to talk to yet another doctor and looked back to make sure Max was resting. His eyes were bulging out of his head! I ran back into the room and ripped the sleep apnea mask from his face. As I did that, he spewed a huge amount of blood from his mouth like a fountain. I remember screaming and being removed from the room. Mama and I waited in the waiting room for what seemed like forever. What could be happening? Surely they would have told us if he died!

Then, another doctor came and introduced himself to us. He was the hematologist. I remember he kept telling me Max's condition was very serious. He kept repeating *very serious.* I finally mustered the courage to ask, "Do you mean I should call the family, serious?". He said yes. I called Max's father and told him he should let Peter know, because Max might not make it through the night. They arrived shortly after, and we all sat together, not knowing anything about TTP or if my sweet husband could survive.

When we were finally allowed to see Max, Peter and I walked back to his room. We stood outside; Peter wouldn't go in. Max had been intubated, he had machines everywhere. There were IV stands with full bags on either side of him. The only thing Peter said to me was, "My parents shouldn't see him this way," as he walked back to the waiting room.

That night, I went home alone and terrified. I had the house phone and my cellphone by my bedside. I sat straight up in bed at four a.m. and looked at the phone. There had been no calls. I remember thinking, "Thank God he didn't die last night." I called the nurses' station and they said he was stable. I got dressed and went directly to the hospital.

As soon as I sat down beside Max, he reached for my

hand. He knew I was there! He was intubated, unconscious, and so very sick, but he knew I was there! I sat with Max all day, every day. Whenever I left, I instructed the nurses to tell Max that I was coming back. I only left for a short time. I didn't want him to think I would leave him there like his ex did when he was in a coma in Germany. I wanted him to know how much I loved him and that I wouldn't leave him!

Max's mother came later and tried to hold Max's hand, but he slapped it away. His father came and sat at his bedside, quietly, not saying much. Friends and family came, shocked to see my big, strong husband full of tubes and surrounded by machines. Some prayed over him, some cried, most had no idea what to say or think. It was times like these that I become invincible. Stronger and more resilient than usual. I had to stay strong for my husband. He needed me and God knows I needed him!

Max's coming days were filled with overcoming this illness. Four hours of dialysis every other day, and three hours of plasmapheresis after that. At least seven hours three times a week hooked up to machines to keep him alive. But, he was alive!

———

Recovery from this horrendous disease was slow. Regular physical therapy to teach Max to walk again. Occupational therapy to help him learn to feed himself, dial the phone, and dress himself. Speech therapy after intubation was removed to ensure he could speak and swallow normally.

Max was eventually moved back to a regular room and then released to come home. He still had to endure months of outpatient dialysis and plasmapherisis. After 3 months on this treatment, the nephrologist walked up to Max and told him he "graduated". His kidneys were healing and he was not going to need any more dialysis. His kidneys would always be slightly compromised, but he would live and continue to get stronger!

CHAPTER **EIGHT**

I talked to my brother, Peter, a few days ago. It was nice to have reconnected after so many years of not having talked. I doubt we will ever be good friends, though.

Just today I have realized that my bipolar illness will never disappear from my body and soul. I have felt like someone stepped into my body and started to wreak havoc on me. It is always a horrible feeling, gives me a headache, and makes me feel numb all over.

I'm finally seeing a new psychologist, and she fits well with me and my problems. Just last week I was feeling suicidal. I started to plan on how I was going to kill myself. I think it is the drugs that make me feel this way. I really didn't want to hurt myself, but the therapist urged me to get an evaluation at a local hospital near where I live. The decision is based on if someone decides to kill himself in the last 48 hours, he may need to talk to someone in intake.

I talked about this three days earlier. I should have gone to adult day group therapy from nine to three, Monday through Friday, and to the doctor on staff. I didn't go, as I knew all too well what it's like to be committed again. They were not going to do this to me again.

If you are ever committed, hang in there. Time heals all wounds. Use the time to think, get well, and take the medication they give you. We all must be responsible and take our meds. Do it for yourself, your family, and your dearest friends.

It seems that self-abuse is happening more frequently now, slapping myself in the face for stupid stuff. I feel so responsible for my mistakes. I know that I'm not perfect, but I try to be. It bothers me that my other family didn't even call me when my father died—like Aunt Greta or her children. Screw them all. My mother has only Alicia and me to watch over her. They put her in area with a higher level of care, as her dementia is becoming more aggressive and making her more dependent on others. I gave them supplements for my mother to take; they're supposed to slow down the dementia. If I lost my mother, I would be devastated.

She is forgetting more now, and it kills me that my brother threw everything of my father's away—his wallet, his driver's license, his leather jacket, and other personal things that he wanted me to have. Peter had told our father that he'd give the things to me that our father had promised me, but he threw so much away. To Peter, my father was a burden. It was Peter who wanted to put him in a nursing home, but my father wouldn't go. He chose to die.

What bothered me the most was Peter's wife went to visit my mother and she then told my father that my mother was faking it. What on earth was she thinking? My mother would not be sitting in a memory care facility for the rest of her life, because she was faking it!

I am definitely not my father's son. My glands are so swollen in my neck that they hurt. My father wouldn't think twice about going to the hospital. I'm only afraid to go because there are so many flu cases. My father was as tough as they came. I miss him very much, which might sound crazy for as brutal as he was to me. He had an interesting life, and sometimes he was easy to talk to. He'd tell you the darnedest stories about his life.

My father, until the day he died, was still aware of his surroundings, and his mind was sharp. I had spent many times alone with my father in the hospital. I have his voice on my cellphone as to proof of what he wanted me to have. Even now I miss him so much. I have the urn with his ashes as a reminder of him. Sadly, I was not with him when he left this world. I had received a call from Bonnie telling me that he died after 9 p.m. His kidneys could not function anymore without the dialysis. My father was a big man, and he made it to age 83, almost 84. I know he is in Heaven now, even though he didn't believe in God himself.

I have only a few family members who mean anything to me who are left on this earth. In my small family circle, there's only my mother, Alicia, and me.

My brother Peter and I haven't really talked in over seven years. It has been said that Peter is a better liar than

I. He made my parents think I was the liar, when in reality it was he who lied to my mother and father. For this, I shall never forgive him, nor his wife. Life is too precious to think of these awful people who make you sick, and are most toxic.

My wife recently told me that I'm the love of her life and she couldn't live without me. I feel the same way. We are married over 19 years, and it definitely has been a roller-coaster ride with my mood swings, depression, and flying off to Germany twice, once on the medication and once off. I didn't make life easy for Alicia, but she stood by me through it all. No matter what had happened, she always said we could make it work. For this, I love her to the moon and back. This is true love; never ending. Always loving; just the two of us forever. Few people ever really experience this type of love. I'm the luckiest man in the whole world. Yes, I have my weaknesses. I think we all have some. Nobody is perfect. I'm not perfect. The only perfect one is God Himself. I should pray more often. Miracles have happened when one prays. It can be life-changing. I survived almost seven near-death experiences, and I'm still here. Amen to that; God had plans for me to live long enough to tell my story. I know why I am here; I'm just an ordinary man, like you.

I hate it when I get the feeling of being anxious. That feeling can destroy a lot of what makes you who you are. Sometimes, when I know I have to go somewhere, I get stressed just thinking about getting there. I know I need to plan ahead and take my time doing so. I like to get up as early as I can and get to the store or company when it just

opens. Like going to a membership warehouse when people get there right at ten o'clock when they open. It used
to drive me nuts that people are so early like cattle--or a
flock of sheep--waiting for the gate to open. Just standing
around with nothing better to do.

I hope that you find my journal helpful to you, and that it
gives you an insight of how bipolar lurks in your body and
changes your life and relationships. I owe a lot of credit to
really great friends who supported me through the tough
parts of my life, and especially to my wife, Alicia, who
managed to help me through all of my troubles and was
there for me when I needed her the most. Alicia is a special person who you only find once in a lifetime. I would
be lying to close this book without thoughts of love and
courage. Bless all who have read this, and I wish you a
fantastic life ahead.

Printed in the United States
By Bookmasters